ALEF-BET

אָלֶף-בֵּית

A HEBREW PRIMER

ABRAHAM SHUMSKY
PROFESSOR OF EDUCATION
Brooklyn College, The City University of New York

ADAIA SHUMSKY
DIRECTOR, PSYCHOLOGICAL SERVICES
The Great Neck School System, N.Y.

Pictures by Marilyn Bass

*This publication was made possible
by a gift from* EDRYCE *and* EDGAR CADDEN

UNION OF AMERICAN HEBREW CONGREGATIONS

UNION OF AMERICAN HEBREW CONGREGATIONS HEBREW PROGRAM

ALEF-BET

Pre-Primer   אָלֶף-בֵּית

OLAM GADOL

Pre-Primer   עוֹלָם גָדוֹל א׳

     A Big World I

Primer   עוֹלָם גָדוֹל ב׳

     A Big World II *(text and workbook/record)*

Teacher's Guide   מַדְרִיךְ לַמוֹרֶה

MAH TOV

Volume I   עֲשׂוֹת מִשְׁפָּט

     Do Justice *(text and workbook)*

Volume II   אַהֲבַת חֶסֶד

     Love Mercy *(text and workbook)*

Volume III   הַצְנֵעַ לֶכֶת

     Walk Humbly *(text and workbook)*

Teacher's Guides   מַדְרִיכִים לַמוֹרֶה

THE SHMUELI FAMILY

Book One   A Cartoon Adventure   מִשְׁפַּחַת שְׁמוּאֵלִי א׳

Book Two   More Cartoon Adventures   מִשְׁפַּחַת שְׁמוּאֵלִי ב׳

     12 Color-Sound Filmloops of Animated Cartoons

THE AUTHORS

DR. ABRAHAM SHUMSKY is a professor of education at Brooklyn College and the author of several books on education. He recently returned from Israel where he developed a college of education in Beit Berl.

DR. ADAIA SHUMSKY is the director of psychological services and special education for the Great Neck, N.Y., school system. She is a practitioner in the area of family therapy.

The Shumskys are frequent lecturers and consultants to Hebrew schools and Jewish organizations.

THE ARTIST

MARILYN BASS created the art work through a process of paper sculpture, collage, and photography. With her husband, Marvin Goldman, who did the photography, she is equally well known in secular publishing.

ACKNOWLEDGMENTS

The Union of American Hebrew Congregations Hebrew Program is a product of an intensive dialogue between the Joint Commission on Jewish Education and the authors.

We wish to thank the following readers and advisors for their constructive suggestions: Eli Gamliel, Rabbi Bernard H. Mehlman, Eva Pallay, Rabbi Steven M. Reuben, and Rabbi Leonard A. Schoolman. Without their guidance, *Alef-Bet* would not have been possible.

Special thanks go to Mr. Ralph Davis for handling the design and production of *Alef-Bet* and to Mrs. Annette Abramson for the copy editing.

We are most grateful to Rabbi Jack D. Spiro who initiated the Hebrew Program and to Rabbi Daniel B. Syme, the guiding force behind *Alef-Bet*.

Our gratitude to Mr. Charles M. Schulz for the use of his Charlie Brown cartoon which appears in this book and for the poem called "Prayer" by Shlomit Grossberg, age 13, of Jerusalem, from *My Shalom, My Peace*, edited by Jacob Zim and Uriel Ofek and translated by Dov Vardi. Copyright © 1975 by Sabra Books, Tel Aviv. Used with permission of McGraw-Hill Book Company.

This is my first Hebrew book

אָלֶף־בֵּית

My Hebrew name is _____

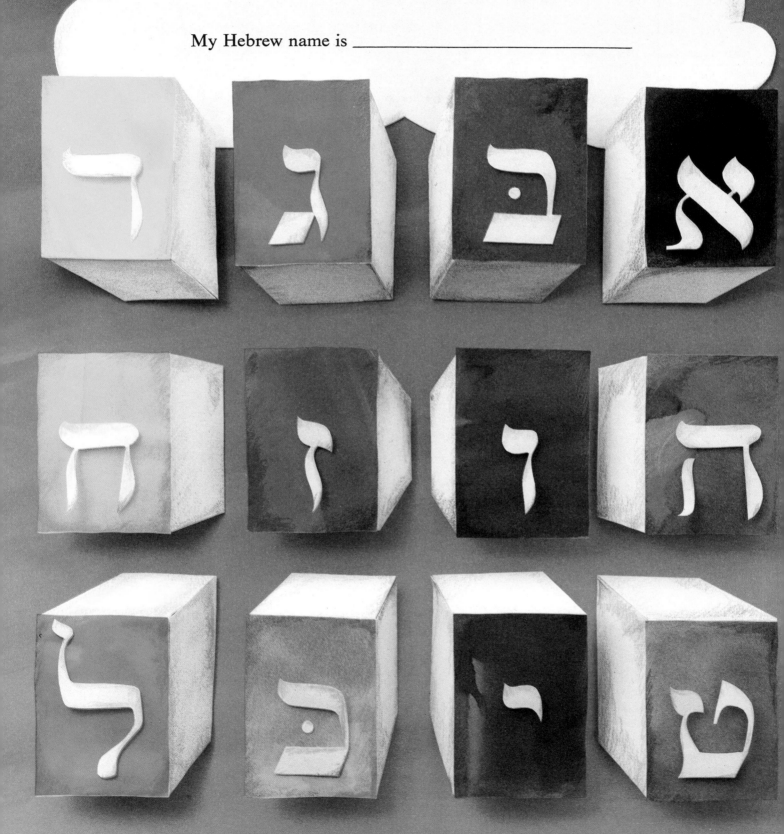

One of the most important inventions was the alphabet. The alphabet makes it possible for us to speak to each other in writing.

Many thousands of years ago, people wrote without using an alphabet. Instead of using letters they used pictures.

When people wanted to write stories about their adventures, they drew beautiful pictures on the walls of the caves where they lived.

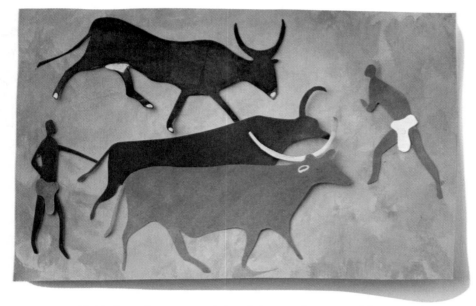

Imagine yourself living in a world without letters. To see how tough it is, "write," without using letters, one of the following: Mazal Tov, Shalom, Happy New Year.

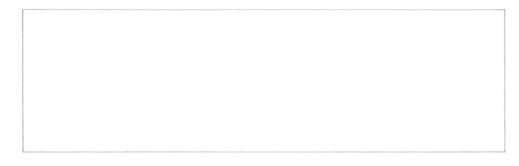

About three thousand years ago, the Hebrews (Jews) and some of their neighbors found a much simpler way to write. They created the letters of the alphabet.

Look at some of the letters.

You will soon learn what they meant to the Hebrews a long time ago.

א – Alef is the first letter in the Hebrew alphabet.
Alef is also an old Hebrew word for a bull.
The picture of the letter א reminded the Hebrews
of the two horns of the bull.

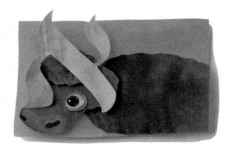

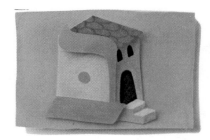

ב – Bet is the second letter in the Hebrew alphabet.
ב reminded the Hebrews of a picture of a house.
In Hebrew, *bayit* means house.

ג – Gimel is the third letter.
It is the first letter of the Hebrew word, *gamal*,
which means camel.
The ג reminded the people of a camel.

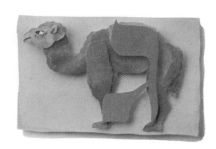

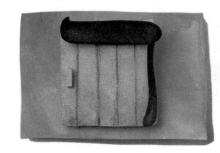

ד – Dalet is the fourth letter.
It looks like a door.
In Hebrew, *dalet* means door.

The Hebrew alphabet is called Alef-Bet. Do you hear the similarity between the words alphabet and Alef-Bet?

The word Alef-Bet came from the names of the first two letters of the Hebrew alphabet, א (*Alef*) and ב (*Bet*).

3

An important rule:

Unlike English which is read from left to right, Hebrew is read from right to left.

1. Here is a line of numbers in English written from left to right:

$1 \rightarrow 2 \rightarrow 3 \rightarrow 4 \rightarrow 5 \rightarrow 6$

2. Here are the same numbers written the way Hebrew is read, from right to left:

$6 \leftarrow 5 \leftarrow 4 \leftarrow 3 \leftarrow 2 \leftarrow 1$ ←———start here

3. Fill in the missing numbers.

—— $\leftarrow 5 \leftarrow 4 \leftarrow$ —— $\leftarrow 2 \leftarrow 1$ ←———start here

4. Follow the story the way Hebrew is read.

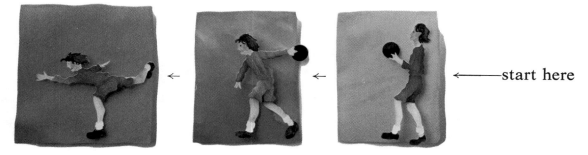

← ← ←———start here

5. Now follow this story according to the numbers.

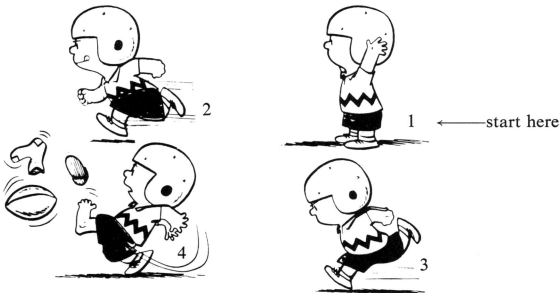

Right to left. Got it? Good! Now let's go on.

4

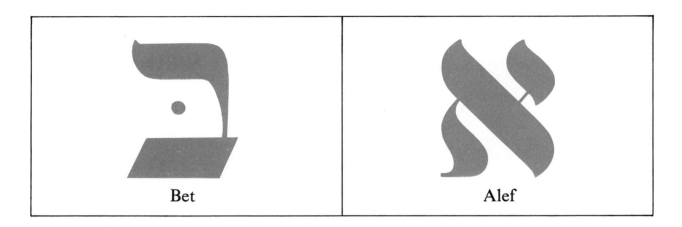

| Bet | Alef |

1 This is the first letter of the Alef-Bet א
It is called Alef א

This is the second letter of the Alef-Bet בּ
It is called Bet בּ
It has the sound of B as in Bar Mitzvah and Bat Mitzvah.

2 Circle the letter Alef.

א בּ א א בּ א בּ א בּ (א)   ⟵——start here

Circle the letter Bet.

בּ בּ א א בּ א בּ א (בּ) א   ⟵——start here

3 How many times does the letter א appear in the following line?

א א א בּ בּ בּ בּ א א א   ⟵——start here

_____times

How many times does the letter בּ appear in the following line?

בּ א בּ א בּ א בּ א בּ א   ⟵——start here

_____times

4 The letter **א** is written this way:

first this　＼

then this　＼⫽

then this　⫽＼

Practice writing the first part.

___ ___ ___ ___ ＼ ＼ ←——start here

Practice writing the first and second parts.

___ ___ ___ ___ ＼/ ＼/ ←——start here

Practice writing the whole **א**.

___ ___ ___ ___ א א ←—— start here

5 The letter **ב** is written this way:

first this　⊐↓

then this　⊐→

Practice writing the first part.

___ ___ ___ ___ ⌐ ⌐ ←——start here

Practice writing the whole **ב**.

___ ___ ___ ___ ⊐ ⊐ ←——start here

6 Practice writing both **א** and **ב**.

___ ___ ___ ___ ⊐ א ←——start here

7 Learn these words.

comes (*ba*) בָּא　　　　father (*aba*) אָבָא

6

8 Connect the sentence with the correct picture.

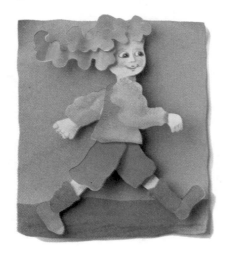

אַבָּא בָּא

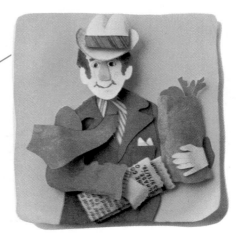

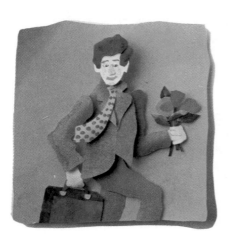

אַבָּא בָּא

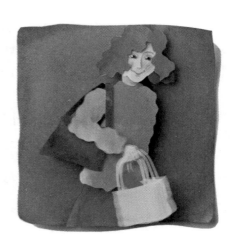

9 Trace all the Alef letters with a colored pencil.

בָּא אַבָּא

Trace the Bet letters with another color.

בָּא אַבָּא

10 The letter Bet has a sister called Vet ב

Vet has the sound of V as in Tel Aviv.

Here are the two sisters ב and בּ

11 Circle the letter Vet.

ב בּ א ב ב ב בּ א   ←——start here

7

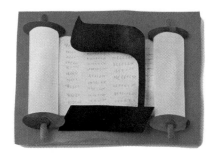
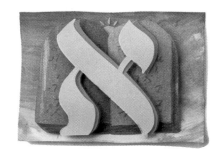

Who Shall Be First?

The first word in the Torah begins with the letter בּ.

Bereshit bara Elohim

בְּרֵאשִׁית בָּרָא אֱלֹהִים

In the beginning God created

Why was the letter בּ and not א chosen to be the first letter in the Bible?
A legend tells us that the letter א felt hurt for being left out.
It thought that it deserved to be first.

Alef, the first letter in the Alef-Bet, came before God and said:

Why did you choose the second letter to be the first letter of the Torah?
Don't I deserve to be the first letter in the creation?

God said to Alef:

בּ stands for בַּיִת (*bayit*), home.
It stands for shelter to the family and for protection.
I want the people of Israel to know that the Torah will give them shelter.
I want them to know that only when they learn the Torah and understand
what is right and what is wrong will they know how to get along in the world.

Alef stood with its head down, ashamed of having asked to be the first.

Then God said to Alef:

I will make you the first letter in the Ten Commandments.

Anochi Adonai Elohecha

אָנֹכִי אֲדֹנָי אֱלֹהֶיךָ

I am the Lord thy God

8

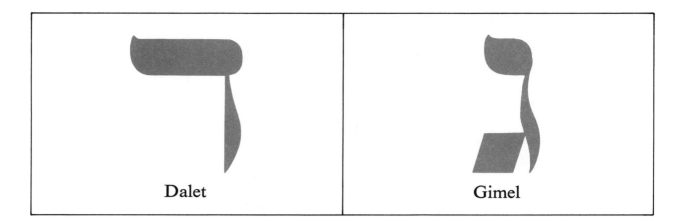

Dalet	Gimel

1 This is the third letter of the Alef-Bet ג
It is called Gimel ג
It has the sound of G as in Haggadah.

This is the fourth letter of the Alef-Bet ד
It is called Dalet ד
It has the sound of D as in David.

2 Circle the letter Gimel.

ד ג ב א   א ב ג ד   ד ג ב א

Circle the letter Dalet.

ד ב ד א   ד ג ד ג   ד ג ב א

3 How many times does the letter ג appear in the following lines?

_____ times   ג א ד ג ב א

_____ times   ג ד ב ד ג ב

How many times does the letter ד appear in the following lines?

_____ times   ד ג ד ב א

_____ times   ד ב ד ד א

9

4 The letter ג is written this way :

first this ⃗↓

then this ↗

Practice writing the first part.

_____ _____ _____ _____ ⃛ ⃛ ⃟ ⃟

Practice writing the whole ג.

_____ _____ _____ _____ ⃛ ⃟

5 The letter ד is written this way :

first this ⃗

then this ⃓↓

Practice writing the first part.

_____ _____ _____ _____ ⃛ ⃟

Practice writing the whole ד.

_____ _____ _____ _____ ⃛ ⃟

6 Practice writing both ג and ד.

_____ _____ _____ _____ ⃛ ⃟

_____ _____ _____ _____ ⃛ ⃟

7 Learn these words.

Haggadah (*Haggadah*) הַגָּדָה   fish (*dag*) דָּג   big (*gadol*) גָּדוֹל

8 Circle the correct word.

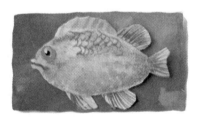

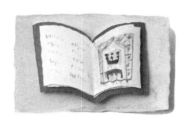

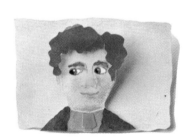

דָּג הַגָּדָה אַבָּא   אַבָּא הַגָּדָה דָּג   אַבָּא הַגָּדָה דָּג

9 Connect the sentence with the correct picture.

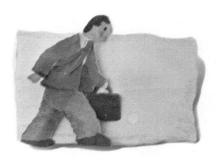

אַבָּא גָּדוֹל

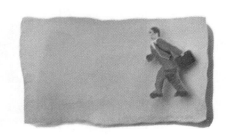

דָּג גָּדוֹל

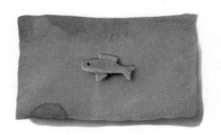

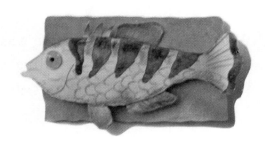

10 Read aloud:

אַבָּא בָּא	אַבָּא גָּדוֹל
דָּג גָּדוֹל	אַבָּא גָּדוֹל בָּא

11 Circle the letter Gimel.

אַבָּא בָּא   דָּג בָּא   הַגָּדָה   גָּדוֹל

12 Trace all the Dalet letters.

הַגָּדָה דָּג גָּדוֹל בָּא אַבָּא גָּדוֹל בָּא

13 Add the missing letter in each square.

א	אַבָּא		בָּ ☐		א	אַבָּא		אַבָּ ☐
ב	אַבָּא		א ☐		ב	בָּא		☐ א
ג	דָּג		☐ דָּ		ג	גָּדוֹל		☐ דוֹל
ד	דָּג		☐ גָּ		ד	גָּדוֹל		☐ וֹל

11

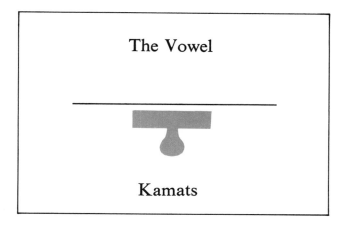

The Vowel

_____

Kamats

When the Hebrew Alef-Bet was invented about three thousand years ago, it had only 22 letters. The Greeks borrowed these letters but found something strange. All the letters were consonants. There were no vowels.

Can you read English without vowels?

Try to read the English   r d.

Some people will read it as *road*, others as *red*, and others as *ride*.

The Greeks had to invent special letters for vowels. The English language, which came from the Greek, has two types of letters, consonants and vowels.

1   Circle the vowels in each of the following:

H a g g a d a h   Y o m   K i p p u r   R o s h   H a s h a n a h

Hebrew has vowels, too. But, unlike English, most Hebrew vowels are not special letters. They are dots and lines. Here are some examples:

אַבָּא גָדוֹל
הַגָּדָה

אַבָּא בָּא
דָג גָדוֹל

12

2 This is the vowel Kamats ָ

Circle the vowel Kamats ָ .

דָּג גָּדוֹל בָּא   אַבָּא גָּדוֹל בָּא

דָּ גָּ בָּ אָ   דָּ גָּ בָּ אָ

3 When you write ָ under the letter א, you get אָ which has the sound Ah.
When you write ָ under the letter בּ, you get בָּ which has the sound Bah.

When you write ָ under the letter גּ, you get גָּ which has the sound Gah.
When you write ָ under the letter דּ, you get דָּ which has the sound Dah.

4 Circle the sound Bah.

דָּ בָּ גָּ אָ   בָּ דָּ גָּ אָ

Circle the sound Ah.

אָ בָּ אָ דָּ   גָּ בָּ אָ אָ

Circle the sound Gah.

הָ גָּ בָּ אָ   גָּ דָּ בָּ אָ גָּ

Circle the sound Dah.

דָּ גָּ בָּ אָ   דָּ גָּ בָּ אָ

5 Match the two columns.

Bah   אָ
Ah   בָּ
Dah   גָּ
Gah   דָּ

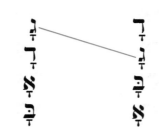

13

6 Read twice:

אָ בָּ גָ דָ   אָ בָּ גָ דָ   אָ בָּ גָ דָ

Let's make it more complicated. Read:

אָאָ	בָּבָ	גָּ	דָד
אָבָּ	בָּאָ	גָד	דָגָ
אָבָּגָ	גָבָּאָ	דָאָבָּ	

7 Practice writing אָ.

— — — — — אָ

Practice writing בָּ.

— — — — — בָּ

Practice writing גָ.

— — — — — גָ

Practice writing דָ.

— — — — — דָ

8 Match the two columns.

אָבָּ	אָבָּ	בָּבָ	אָאָ
אָד	אָגָ	אָאָ	בָּבָ
אָגָ	אָד	דָד	גָּ
דָאָ	דָאָ	גָּ	דָד

14

```
┌─────────────────────────────────┐
│           The Vowel             │
│                                 │
│         _____             │
│           �█████                │
│                                 │
│           Patach                │
└─────────────────────────────────┘
```

1 You already know the vowel Kamats ָ.

It is written under the letter.

אָ with ָ is אָ which has the sound Ah.

בּ with ָ is בָּ which has the sound Bah.

גּ with ָ is __ which has the sound Gah.

דּ with ָ is __ which has the sound Dah.

2 The vowel Kamats ָ has a sister called Patach ַ.

It is also written under the letter.

Circle the vowel Patach.   הַגָּדָה   אַבָּא

3 The vowel ַ generally gives the letter the same sound as does the ָ.

אַ אָ Both have the sound Ah.

בַּ בָּ Both have the sound Bah.

גַּ גָּ Both have the sound ____.

דַּ דָּ Both have the sound ____.

15

4 Read these sounds:

גַ גַ גַ   גָ גָ גָ | אַ אַ אַ   אָ אָ אָ

דָ דַ דַ   דָ דָ דָ | בַ בַ בַ   בָ בָ בָ

5 The vowel Kamats ָ and the vowel Patach ַ are a pair.

They sound alike. Match the pair vowels.

אַאַ   אָאָ   בַ אַ דַ גָ   אָ בָ גָ דָ

גַ   בָבָ

דָדָ   גָגָ

בָבָ   דַדַ

6 Ask your teacher to write your name in Hebrew.

Is there a ָ in your name?   Yes ☐   No ☐

Is there a ַ in your name?   Yes ☐   No ☐

16

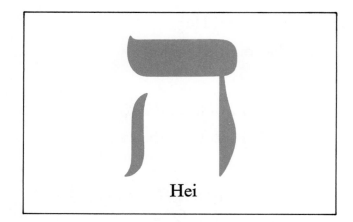

Hei

1 This is the fifth letter of the Alef-Bet ה

It is called Hei ה

It has the sound of H as in Hello and Hamotzi.

2 Circle the letter Hei.

הַגָּדָה   גבההדג   אבדהג   אבגדה

3 How many times did the letter ה appear in the line above?

_____times

4 The letter ה is written this way:

first this ה↓

then this ↓ה

Practice writing the first part.

___   ___   ___   ___   ___   ⁝   ┐

Practice writing the whole ה.

___   ___   ___   ___   ⁝   ⊓

17

5   ה with ָ is הָ which has the sound Hah.

  ה with ַ is הַ which has the sound Hah.

  א with ָ is אָ; א with ַ is אַ. Both have the sound Ah.

  בּ with ָ is בָּ; בּ with ַ is בַּ. Both have the sound ____.

  ג with ָ is גָ; ג with ַ is __. Both have the sound Gah.

  ד with ָ is דָ; ד with ַ is דַ. Both have the sound ____.

  ה with ָ is הָ; ה with ַ is __. Both have the sound Hah.

6   Read these sounds:

בְּהָ	אָהָ	אָהָ	הָ	הַ	הָ
הַבְּ	הַדָ	הַדָ	בָּהַ	בָּהַ	בָּהַ
הַגָ	גָהַ	הַגָ	הַדְבָּ	הַדָ	גָהָ
אַבָּא	אַבָּא	אַבָּא	בָּא	בָּא	בָּא

7   Circle the sounds on the left which match the sound on the right.

הַ	בָּ	הָ	א	הָ	אָ		הָ
בַ	הָ	בָּ	אָ	הַ	אָ		א
אָ	הָ	הַ	א	הַ	בָּ		הָ
הָ	א	אָ	הַ	דַ	גָ		אָ
בָּ	א	בָּ	הַ	הָ	גָ		בָּ
דַ	אָ	הָ	דָ	דַ	הָ		דָ
ג	הַ	דָ	גָ	בָּ	אָ		גָ

18

8 Here are five Hebrew words:

הַגָּדָה   דָג   בָּא   אַבָּא   גָּדוֹל

How many times does the letter א appear in these words?

_____ times

How many times does the letter בּ appear in these words?

_____ times

How many times does the letter ג appear in these words?

_____ times

How many times does the letter ד appear in these words?

_____ times

How many times does the letter ה appear in these words?

_____ times

9 Read aloud:

הַ   הַ   הַ

הַגָּ   הַגָּ   הַגָּ

הַגָּדָה   הַגָּדָה   הַגָּדָה

10 Write in each box the missing letter and vowel in הַגָּדָה.

הַ ☐ דָה

☐ גָדָה

ה ☐ הַגָּ

☐ גָד ☐

11 Trace the letter Hei ה.

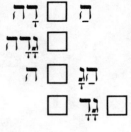

Trace the sound Hah.

19

The Story of the Haggadah הַגָּדָה

The הַגָּדָה is read during the Pesach seder. The הַגָּדָה is a collection of stories, prayers, and songs. It tells about the Jews in Egypt who were slaves to Pharaoh and how they came out of Egypt to freedom.

As we chant the הַגָּדָה and eat the *matzah*, we remember the sufferings of the Jewish people in the past and present. We hope and pray for freedom.

It is said in the Haggadah:
"In every generation, every Jew should see himself as if he were redeemed from slavery in Egypt...."

In every generation the הַגָּדָה is published with new illustrations. Can you find an illustrated הַגָּדָה and share it with your class?

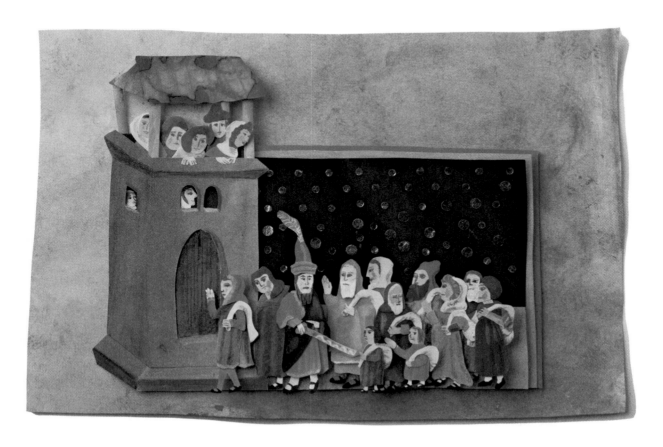

The Vowel	The Vowel
Segol	Tserei

1 Most Hebrew vowels come in pairs.

A pair of vowels sounds alike.

You already know one pair: Kamats ָ and Patach ַ

אָ and אַ have the sound Ah.

בָּ and בַּ have the sound Bah.

גָ and גַ have the sound ____ .

דָ and דַ have the sound ____ .

הָ and הַ have the sound ____ .

2 In modern Hebrew the vowels Kamats ָ and Patach ַ have a similar sound.

Here is a new pair of vowels: Tserei ֵ and Segol ֶ

א with ֵ is אֵ; א with ֶ is אֶ. Both have the sound Eh.

ב with ֵ is בֵּ; ב with ֶ is בֶּ. Both have the sound Beh.

ג with ֵ is __ ; ג with ֶ is גֶ. Both have the sound Geh.

ד with ֵ is דֵ; ד with ֶ is __ . Both have the sound Deh.

ה with ֵ is __ ; ה with ֶ is __ . Both have the sound Heh.

21

3 Read these sounds:

דֵ גֶ דֵ גֵ | אָ אָ אֶ אַ
דֶ גֵ דֶ גָ | אֵ אֵ אֶ אַ
הֶ דֵ הֵ דֶ | בֶ בֵ בֵ בָ
הֶ דֶ הֶ דֵ | בֶ בֵ בֶ בֵ

Now let's make it more complicated. Read these sounds:

אֵה אֶד | אֵג אֵב
בֵה בֵג | בֵד בָא
גֶ א חֵג | בֵג גֵד
הֵב בֵה | הֵד הֵה

4 Connect the sound in the middle with the same sounds on the outside.

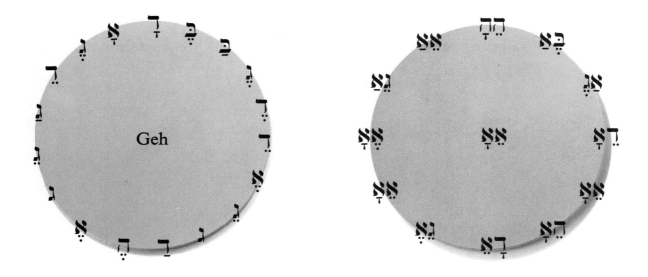

5 Circle the sounds on the left which match the sound on the right.

אָבְ אָבְ אָג אֶרְ | אֶבְ

אֶרְ אֶרְ אַה אָג | אֶרְ

אֶה אֶרְ אֶה אָג | אֶה

בֶּבְ בֶּה בֶּבְ בֶּבְ | בֶּבְ

דֵּבְ בֵּרְ בֶּבְ בָּא | בָּא

גַּג גֶּג גַּג גֶּג | גֶּג

דֶּד דָּד דֵּד דֵּד | דֵּד

הֵה הָה הֵה הֵה | הֵה

גֶּג גַּג גֵּג גַּג | גַּג

דַּד דֵּד דֵּד דֵּג | דֵּד

6 You now know five letters:

ה   ד   ג   ב   א

You now know two pairs of vowels:

Kamats ָ   Patach ַ

Tserei ֵ   Segol ֶ

7 You can read:

אַבָּא בָּא   דָּג בָּא

אַבָּא גָדוֹל   דָג גָדוֹל

אַבָּא גָדוֹל בָּא   דָג גָדוֹל בָּא

הַגָּדָה

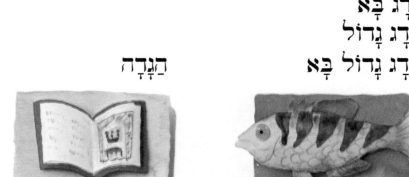
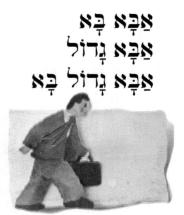

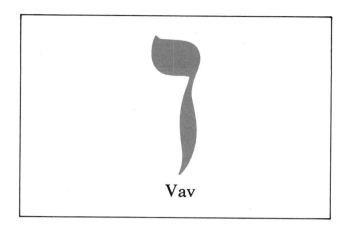

Vav

1 This is the sixth letter of the Alef-Bet ו

It is called Vav ו

It has the sound of V as in Bar Mitzvah and Bat Mitzvah.

2 Circle the letter Vav.

א ב ג ד ה ו   ב ה ד ו ג א

א ב ג ד ה ו   ב ה ו ד א

א ב ג ד ה ו   ודג בו או

3 How many times did the letter ו appear in the lines above?

_____ times

4 The letter ו is written this way:

first this   ־ʾ

then this   ו↓

Practice writing the ו.

___   ___   ___   ___   ו⋮   ו

24

5 The letter ו, like many other Hebrew letters, is a picture of a word.

The word Vav means a hook, an object used to connect one thing to another.

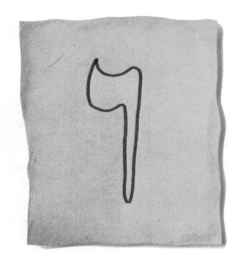

Decorate the letter ו.

6 ו with ◌ָ is וָ ; ו with ◌ַ is וַ. Both have the sound Vah.

א with ◌ָ is אָ; א with ◌ַ is אַ. Both have the sound Ah.

ב with ◌ָ is בָ; ב with ◌ַ is בַ. Both have the sound Bah.

ג with ◌ָ is ___; ג with ◌ַ is גַ. Both have the sound ____.

ד with ◌ָ is דָ; ד with ◌ַ is ___. Both have the sound ____.

ה with ◌ָ is הָ; ה with ◌ַ is הַ. Both have the sound ____.

ו with ◌ָ is וָ ; ו with ◌ַ is ___. Both have the sound Vah.

7 Match.

Vah	אָ	בַ	אָ
Bah	בָ	אַ	בַ
Ah	ו	ג	גַ
Hah	דָ	הָ	דָ
Dah	הָ	ו	הָ
Vah	וַ	דַ	וַ

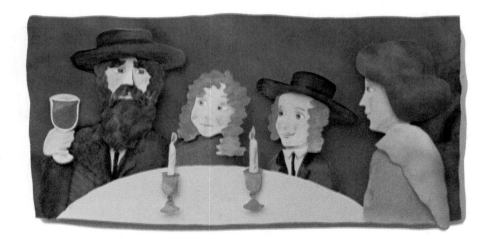

8 The *Kiddush* is a blessing recited on Friday evening as we begin the Shabbat.

This blessing is recited over a full glass of wine while all the family members gather around the table.

The *Kiddush* tells the story of God completing the creation of the world on the sixth day and creating the Shabbat as a day of rest.

Now listen to your teacher read part of the *Kiddush* in Hebrew.

See if you can recognize the sound of וֹ as your teacher reads the *Kiddush*.

וַיְהִי עֶרֶב וַיְהִי בֹקֶר יוֹם הַשִּׁשִּׁי.
וַיְכֻלּוּ הַשָּׁמַיִם וְהָאָרֶץ וְכָל צְבָאָם
וַיְכַל אֱלֹהִים בַּיּוֹם הַשְּׁבִיעִי.
מְלַאכְתּוֹ אֲשֶׁר עָשָׂה.

Look at the prayer again and circle the sound וָ.

9 ו with ֶ is וֶ; ו with ֵ is וֵ. Both have the sound Veh.

א with ֶ is __; א with ֵ is __.

ב with ֵ is בֵ. It has the sound _____.

ג with ֶ is __. It has the sound _____.

ו with ֵ is __. It has the sound _____.

ו with ֶ is __. It has the sound Veh.

10 Circle those pairs of letters which do not sound the same.

וֶאֵ	וֶאֶ	וֶאֵ		וַוֵ	וֵוֶ	וֶוֵ
בֵוַ	בֶוֵ	בֶוַ		וֵוַ	וֶוֵ	וַוֵ
גֵוַ	גַוֵ	גַוֶ		וֶוֵ	וֵוֵ	וֵוֶ
וֵהֵ	וֶהֵ	וֵהֶ		וֶוֵ	וֵוֶ	וֶוֵ

11 Check the lines where the letters are in correct alphabetical order.

אֶ בֵּ דָּ גֵ הָ וֶ ☐	א ב ג ד ו ה ☐
אֶ בֵּ גָ דֵ הֶ וֶ ☐	א ב ג ד ה ו ☐
אֶ בֵּ גֵ הֶ דֵ וֶ ☐	אָ בֵ גַ דָ הָ וֶ ☐
אֶ בֵּ גֵ דֶ הֵ וֶ ☐	אָ גַ בָ דָ הָ וֶ ☐

12 Do you remember the letter Vet?

ב with ָ is בָ; ו with ָ is וָ. Both have the sound Vah.

ב with ֵ is בֵ; ו with ֵ is __. Both have the sound Veh.

Vet and Vav are two *different* letters that *sound* alike.

13 ב with ַ is בַ; ו with ַ is וַ. Both have the sound Vah.

ב with ֶ is בֶ; ו with ֶ is וֶ. Both have the sound ____.

27

וְ	יַלְדָה	יֶלֶד
and	girl	boy

1 Learn these words.

and (*ve*) וְ   girl (*yaldah*) יַלְדָה   boy (*yeled*) יֶלֶד

2 Circle the correct word.

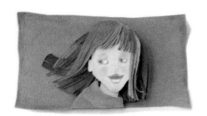

אַבָּא   יַלְדָה   יֶלֶד

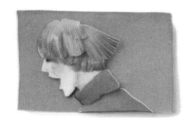

אַבָּא   יַלְדָה   יֶלֶד

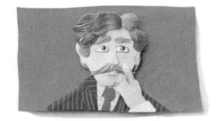

אַבָּא   יֶלֶד   יַלְדָה

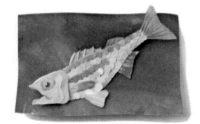

דָג   יֶלֶד   יַלְדָה

3 Check the correct answer.

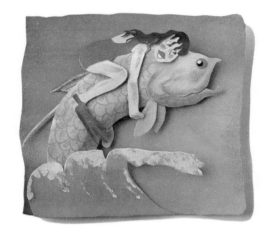

☐ יֶלֶד וְיַלְדָה
☐ יַלְדָה וְאַבָּא
☐ יַלְדָה וְדָג
☐ יֶלֶד וְאַבָּא

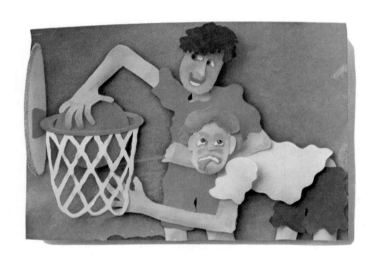

☐ יֶלֶד גָּדוֹל וְיַלְדָה
☐ יֶלֶד גָּדוֹל וְאַבָּא
☐ יֶלֶד גָּדוֹל וְדָג גָּדוֹל
☐ יֶלֶד גָּדוֹל וְיֶלֶד גָּדוֹל

4 Read aloud:

אַבָּא בָּא	יֶלֶד גָּדוֹל בָּא
אַבָּא גָּדוֹל בָּא	יֶלֶד וְדָג גָּדוֹל
	יֶלֶד וְיַלְדָה

5 Circle the vowel Segol ֶ

אֶ בֶּ גֶּ דֶ הֶ וֶ   יֶלֶד   יַלְדָה

29

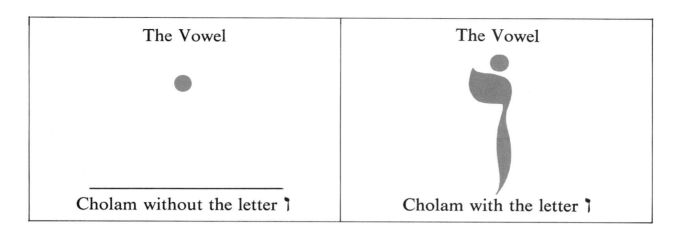

The Vowel	The Vowel
●	וֹ
Cholam without the letter ו	Cholam with the letter ו

1 You know two pairs of vowels:

Kamats ָ and Patach ַ sound alike.

Tserei ֵ and Segol ֶ sound alike.

Both pairs are written under the letter:

בֵ בֶ   בַ בָ

2 Here is a new pair of vowels: בוֹ and בֹ.

This pair is written above the line.

The vowels וֹ and ֹ sound alike.

They have the sound of o as in

more, Rosh Hashanah, and Yom Kippur.

3 א with וֹ is אוֹ; א with ֹ is אֹ. Both have the sound Oh.

ב with וֹ is בוֹ; ב with ֹ is בֹ. Both have the sound Boh.

ג with וֹ is גוֹ; ג with ֹ is גֹ. Both have the sound _____.

ר with וֹ is ___; ר with ֹ is רֹ. Both have the sound _____.

ה with וֹ is הוֹ; ה with ֹ is ___. Both have the sound Hoh.

ו with וֹ isווֹ; ו with ֹ is וֹ. Both have the sound Voh.

30

4 Practice writing וֹ.

___ ___ ___ ___ וֹ וֹ

Practice writing Cholam without Vav.

___ ___ ___ ___ ___ ֹ

Try it with the letter בֹ.

___ ___ ___ ___ בֹ בֹ

___ ___ ___ ___ בֹ בֹ

5 Match.

Goh	אוֹ	גֹ		אוֹ
Oh	בֹ	אֹ		בוֹ
Boh	גוֹ	בֹ		גוֹ
Hoh	דֹ	הֹ		דוֹ
Voh	הֹ	וֹ		הוֹ
Doh	ווֹ	דֹ		ווֹ

6 Read aloud:

אוֹ אֹ אוֹ   אוֹ בוֹ גוֹ

הוֹ הֹ הוֹ   דוֹ הוֹ ווֹ

ווֹ וֹ ווֹ   אוֹ בוֹ

בֹ בֹ בדוֹ   גוֹ גוֹד

7 Circle the vowel וֹ.

shalom   שָׁלוֹם

Adon Olam   אֲדוֹן עוֹלָם

Yom Kippur   יוֹם כִּפּוּר

big   גָּדוֹל

Circle the vowel ֹ

Rosh Hashanah   רֹאשׁ הַשָּׁנָה

8 Connect the sounds which make a pair.

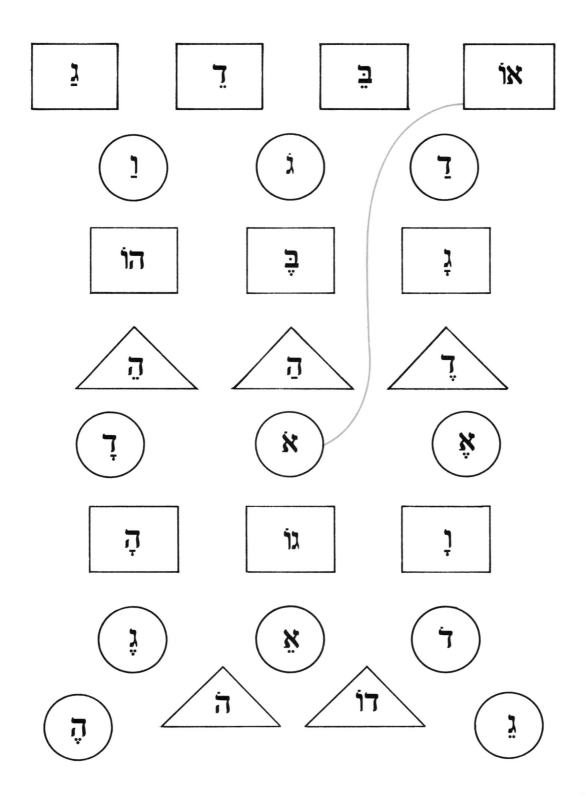

32

9 Make cards like those you see on this page. Put them together to make as many words as you can.

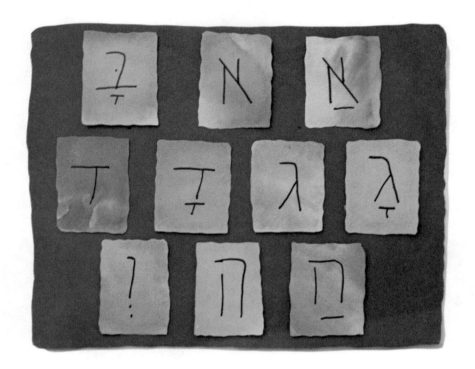

How many words did you make? _____

10 Write some of the words here:

fish

father

comes

Haggadah

11 Connect the correct word with the pictures.

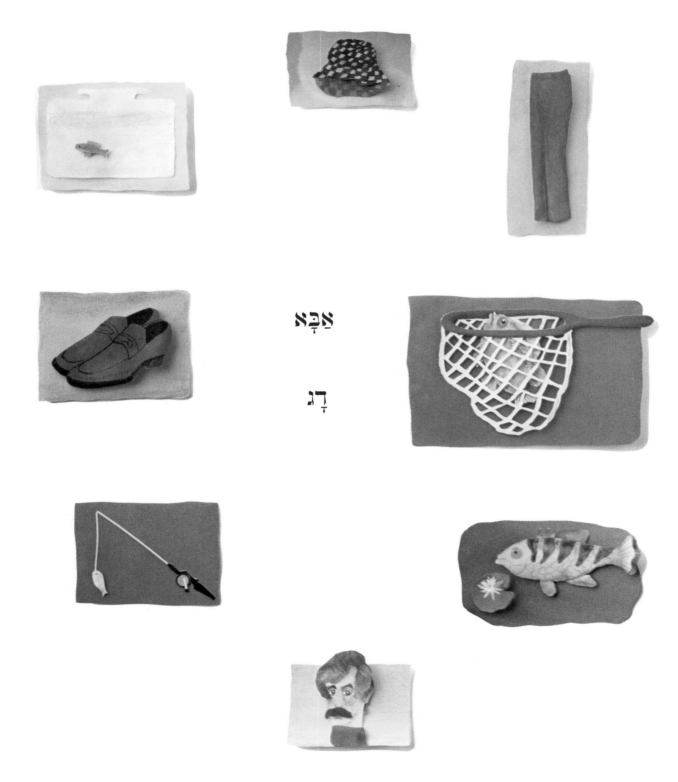

אַבָּא

דָג

The Vowel	The Vowel
ּ ּ ּ	וּ
Kubuts	Shuruk

1 Most Hebrew vowels come in pairs.
Here are the pairs you already know:

Kamats ָ and Patach ַ as in אַ   אָ

Tserei ֵ and Segol ֶ as in אֶ   אֵ

Cholam with וֹ as in גֹו   בֹו   אֹו
Cholam without וֹ as in גֹ   בֹ   אֹ

2 Here is a new pair of vowels:
The vowel וּ (Shuruk) and the vowel ֻ (Kubuts)

In modern Hebrew, the vowel וּ and the vowel ֻ sound alike.
They have the sound oo as in moon or food.

3 The sounds of the vowel וּ and the vowel ֻ appear in the names of some of
the Jewish holidays.

Circle the vowel וּ and the vowel ֻ in these words:

Yom Kippur יוֹם כִּפּוּר   Purim פּוּרִים
Sukot סֻכּוֹת   Shavuot שָׁבוּעוֹת

4 In each line, circle the sound which is different from the others.

בְּ	בְּ	אֶ		אוֹ	בּוּ	אוֹ
דְּ	גְּ	גְּ		גוּ	דוּ	דוּ
דְּ	הְ	דְּ		הוּ	הוּ	ווּ
זְ	גְ	זְ		ווּ	הוּ	ווּ

5 Circle the sounds on the left which match the sound on the right.

בּוּ	בְּ	אֶ		אֶ
דוּ	אוֹ	גוּ		אוֹ
הוּ	גְּ	גוּ		הוּ
ווּ	הְ	דְּ		ווּ

גְּבְּ	בְּבְּ	אְבְּ		בְּבְּ
בְּבְּ	הְבְּ	דְבְּ		בְּבְּ
בְּבְּ	בְּבוּ	בְּבְּ		בְּבוּ
גוּגוֹ	גוֹגוּ	גוּגוֹ		גוּגוֹ

6 Read aloud:

גֵּד	גוּדוֹ	גוּד		אָבְּ	אָבוּ	אָבוֹ
בָּדוּ	בְּדוּ	בּוֹדוֹ		אוֹהוֹ	אוּדוֹ	אוּגוֹ
הָדוּ	הֹדוּ	הוֹדוּ		אוֹוּ	אָדוּ	אָהוּ
דוֹגוּ	דוּגְ	ווֹדְ		בְּהוּ	כָהוּ	בְּדוּ

7 In each line, circle the letter which has a vowel different from the other vowels.

בוּ	גוּ	דוּ	הוּ	אָ	בּוּ	אוֹ
בְּ	וְ	הְ	דְ	גֵ	בְּ	אֶ
וְ	הְ	בּוּ	בְּ	אָ	דְ	גֵ
וֹ	בְּ	אוֹ	אוֹ	דוּ	דְ	הוּ

36

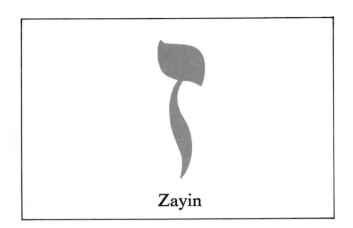

Zayin

1 This is the seventh letter of the Alef-Bet ז

It is called Zayin ז

It has the sound of Z as in Mazal Tov and Mezuzah.

2 Circle the letter Zayin: ז ו ה ד ג ב א   ז ו ה ד ג ב א

3 How many times did the letter ז appear in the line above? _____ times

4 The letter ז is written this way:

first this ⟋

then this זֿ

Practice writing ז.

____   ____   ____   ____   ֻז   זֿ

5 Do not confuse the letter ז with the letter ו.
Circle the letter ז: ו ז   ז ו   ו ז   ז ו

6 ז with ָ is זָ; ז with ַ is זַ. Both have the sound Zah.

ז with ֶ is זֶ; ז with ֵ is __. Both have the sound _____.

ז with וֹ is זוֹ; ז with ֹ is זֹ. Both have the sound _____.

ז with וּ is זוּ; ז with ֻ is __. Both have the sound Zu.

37

מְזוּזָה

Mezuzah

7 Do you know what a מְזוּזָה (*Mezuzah*) is?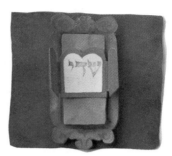
It is customary for every Jewish home to have a מְזוּזָה
on its doorpost. Inside the מְזוּזָה is a small parchment
on which is written the first paragraphs of the *Shema*.

In the past, the מְזוּזָה used to be placed on the doors
of Jewish homes to let travelers know that they could enter without fear.

What things in a house tell you that a Jewish family lives there?

_____

_____

_____

Trace the letter ז in the word מְזוּזָה

Can one of you bring a מְזוּזָה to school and show it to the group?

Can you make a מְזוּזָה?

8 Match.

זְ	זְ	Zah		זָ
זֻ	זַ	Zoh		זֹ
זֹ	זוּ	Zu		זוּ
זַ	זוֹ	Zeh		זוֹ

9 Read aloud:

זַד	זַג	זַב	זוּ	זוֹ	זַ
זָא	זֶ	זֶ	זַדוּ	זַגוּ	זַבוּ
הַזָ	דַז	זָד	זְגוּ	זָדוּ	זֶהוּ
זוּזָה	זוּזָה	זוּז	זָאוֹ	זָאוֹ	זָאוֹ

בָּאִים	בָּאָה	בָּא
come, pl.	comes, f.	comes, m.

1 Study these words.

come, pl. (ba'im) בָּאִים   comes, f. (ba'ah) בָּאָה   comes, m. (ba) בָּא

2 Check the sentence which describes the picture.

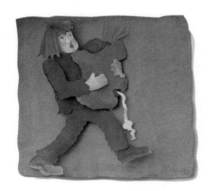

☐ אַבָּא בָּא
☐ יַלְדָּה בָּאָה
☐ יֶלֶד וְיַלְדָּה בָּאִים
☐ יַלְדָּה וְאַבָּא בָּאִים

3 Check the sentence which does not describe the picture.

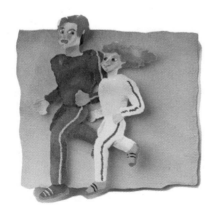

☐ יֶלֶד גָּדוֹל בָּא
☐ יַלְדָּה בָּאָה
☐ דָּג גָּדוֹל בָּא
☐ יֶלֶד וְיַלְדָּה בָּאִים

39

4   Circle the word which is correct for each picture.

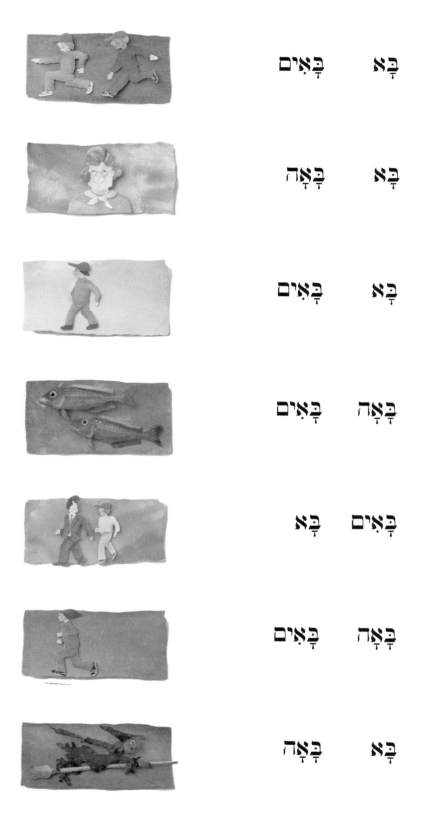

בָּא   בָּאִים

בָּא   בָּאָה

בָּא   בָּאִים

בָּאָה   בָּאִים

בָּאִים   בָּא

בָּאָה   בָּאִים

בָּא   בָּאָה

40

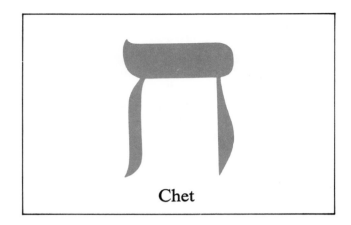

Chet

1 This is the eighth letter of the Alef-Bet ח

It is called Chet ח

You may have some trouble pronouncing the letter. Do you know why?

There is no sound in the English language similar to the sound of ח. It sounds a little like the Ch in Chanukah.

2 Circle the letter Chet.

חָ וֹ זֹ חָ חֶ וֹ זֹ הָ דָ גָ בָ עָ ח וֹ ה ד ג בַּ אַ

3 How many times did the letter ח appear in the line above?

_____ times

4 Check the line where all the sounds are the same.

חָח ☐	חָח	חָח	חָ ☐	חוֹ	חוֹ
חֶח ☐	חֶח	חוֹח	חוֹ ☐	חוֹ	חוֹ
חֶא ☐	חֶא	חֶא	חֶ ☐	חֶ	חֶ
חַר ☐	חוּדוֹ	חוּר	חוֹ ☐	חוֹ	חוֹ

5 On each line, circle the sound which is different from the others.

חָד	חוּד	חָד	חֶ	חֶ	חֶ
חֹג	חוּג	חוּג	חֹ	חָ	חוֹ
חֶבּוֹ	חֶבּוֹ	חֶבּ	חֶ	חֶ	חֶ
בֹּח	בֹּחוּ	בֹּח	חוֹ	ח	ח

41

6 The letter ה is written this way:

first this   →⌐↓

then this   ↓⌐¬

Practice writing the first part.

___ ___ ___ ___ ⫟ ⌐

Practice writing the whole ה.

___ ___ ___ ___ ⫟ ⊓

7 This is the letter Chet   ח

This is the letter Hei   ה

Do you see the difference between them?

How many times does the letter ח appear in the line below?

ח   ח   ה   ח   ה   ח   ח   ה   ח

_____ times

How many times does the letter ה appear in the same line?

_____ times

8 Match.

הֶ	חַ		אוֹ	גוֹ	אָ
דֶ	זַ		גַ	דוֹ	בָ
חֶ	דַ		דַ	בּוֹ	גָ
זֶ	הֵ		אָ	אוֹ	דָ

גַ	דַ		חוֹ	וַ	הַ
	בֵ		וַ	חוֹ	זַ
אֵ	גַ		זַ	הוֹ	זַ
דַ	אָ		חוֹ	זַ	חַ

42

9 Check the line which is in correct alphabetical order.

א ב ג ד ה ה ו ח ז ☐

א ב ג ד ה ה ו ז ח ☐

א ב ד ה ה ג ו ז ח ☐

א ב ג ד ה ה ו ז ח ☐

10 Circle the letter Chet in the words below.

Chanukah   חֲנֻכָּה

Pesach (Passover)   פֶּסַח

holiday   חַג

Chanukah and Pesach are Jewish holidays.

The Hebrew word for holiday is חַג.

11 Look at the word חַג.

Trace both letters.   ג   ח

12 Read aloud:

יֶלֶד וְיַלְדָה בָּאִים	אַבָּא בָּא	חַג בָּא
אַבָּא וְיֶלֶד בָּאִים	יַלְדָה בָּאָה	חַג גָּדוֹל
יַלְדָה וְאַבָּא בָּאִים	יֶלֶד גָּדוֹל בָּא	חַג גָּדוֹל בָּא

43

13 Write the word חַג to the right of each picture.

Then, write the name of the holiday in English to the left of each picture.

Chanukah

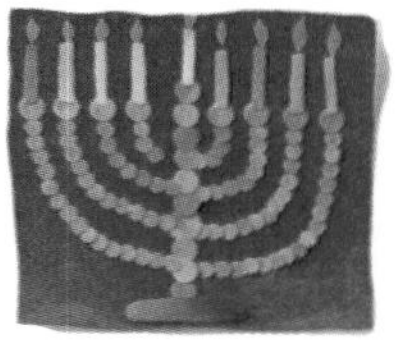

חַג

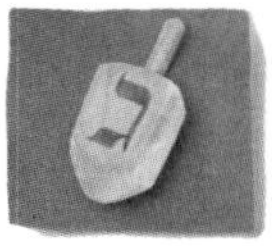

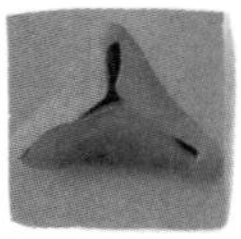

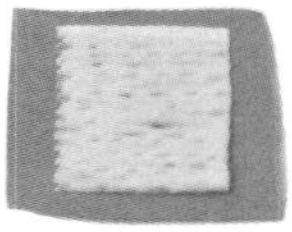

_____

_____

_____

_____

_____

_____

_____

_____

Sukot

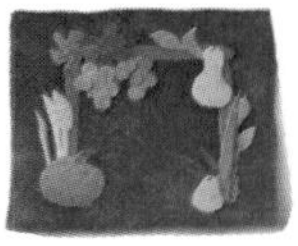

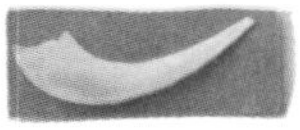

_____

_____

_____

| Chanukah | Pesach | Purim | Rosh Hashanah | Sukot |

44

Chalah 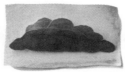	חַלָה

Chalah חַלָה is a word that starts with the letter ח

חַלָה is the braided bread eaten on Shabbat and holidays.

The custom of baking חַלָה goes back to biblical times.

1 Do you know how a חַלָה is baked?

How is it different from ordinary bread? _____

_____

_____

_____

2 Can you bake a חַלָה?

The Shabbat meal begins when the חַלָה is uncovered and the *Hamotzi* blessing is recited.

Listen as your teacher recites the *Hamotzi*:

Baruch Atah	בָּרוּךְ אַתָּה
Adonai Elohenu	אַדֹנָי אֱלֹהֵינוּ
Melech ha'olam	מֶלֶךְ הָעוֹלָם
Hamotzi lechem	הַמוֹצִיא לֶחֶם
Min ha'aretz	מִן הָאָרֶץ

Blessed is
The Lord our God
Ruler of the universe
Who causes bread to come
From the earth

45

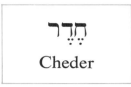

חֶדֶר

Cheder

The famous Hebrew poet Chaim Nachman Bialik was born more than one hundred years ago in a small village in Russia.

The Jewish people in his time followed a tradition which said:

When children are three, teach them the letters.

When children are five, teach them the Torah.

On his third birthday it was time for Chaim to enter the חֶדֶר. In those days, the Hebrew school was called חֶדֶר. It was a room, very often in the home of the teacher, where the children studied from morning till night.

On the first day of school Chaim walked with his father to חֶדֶר. It was early in the morning and the sun had not yet risen. When they reached the חֶדֶר, his father whispered in his ear:

Chaim, pay attention to your teacher.

Maybe one day you will be a rabbi.

Chaim promised to pay attention. He, too, wanted to grow up to be a learned man. But, when the teacher showed him the first letters, Chaim forgot his promise.

Chaim looked at the Alef-Bet and saw beautiful pictures. The letters turned into soldiers marching in a parade. The letter ג looked to him like a soldier beating on a drum; the א looked like a soldier leaning forward with a pack on his back.

As he was looking at the soldiers marching on the page, he heard his teacher:
—What are you looking at, Chaim?
—I am looking at the drummer.
—What drummer? Pay attention, Chaim.
This is Alef. Say Alef אָ.
—Alef אָ.
—Good. Repeat after me again. Alef אָ. Alef אָ.
—Alef אָ, Alef אָ, said Chaim.

46

But as soon as the teacher turned around, the letters changed into pictures again. There was ל which looked like a strange bird stretching its head upward and standing on one leg like an ostrich.

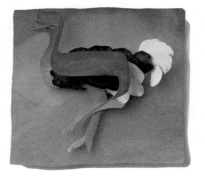

And there was another funny shape, צ, that looked like a bird with fancy feathers perched in a tree. And there he was, Chaim himself, standing on top of a roof ם looking all around, looking at the houses, trees, and animals of the village. And way down near the river was a girl carrying two pails of water.

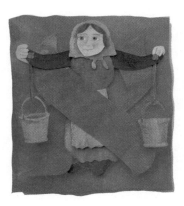

Suddenly, he saw the teacher standing near him, pointing to the letter א:

—Chaim, what is this?

—A girl, carrying two pails of water on her shoulders.

He heard the children behind him laugh and his teacher, in an angry voice, said:

—Chaim, you are not listening. Now pay attention.
Say Kamatz, Alef אָ; Kamatz, Bet בָּ.

—Kamatz, Alef אָ; ָ, Bet בָּ, said Chaim.

Chaim had a hard time learning in the חֶדֶר, but he grew up to be a learned man. His gift for make-believe made him a great poet and storyteller.

47

This song was written in Yiddish one hundred years ago.
It was translated into Hebrew and into English.

It is a song about the חֶדֶר. The children are huddled around a wood
stove, while their teacher, called Rebbe, teaches the Alef-Bet.

In the little stove a fire is burning,
    what a cozy place!
Rebbe teaching children, learning to read
    the Alef-Bet. (Repeat.)

Look here children, think hard, little ones,
    reading has its law.
Say it after me, and keep repeating it:
    Kamatz ◌ָ Alef אָ. (Repeat.)

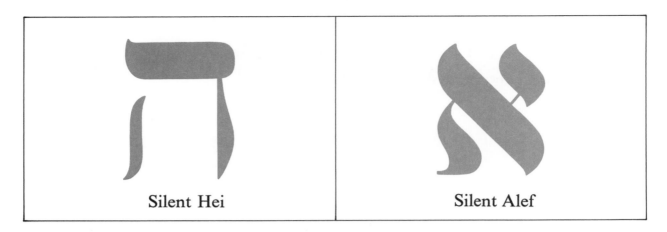

| Silent Hei | Silent Alef |

1 Read aloud: בָּא

Do you hear the א in בָּא? The answer is NO.

The letter א is silent when it has no vowel.

2 Circle the silent Alef in the word אַבָּא

3 Read aloud:

בָּא	בָּא	בָּא	בָּא	בָּא	בָּא
גֵּא	גֵּא	גֵּא	גֵּא	גֵּא	גֵּא
דֶא	דֶא	דֶא	דָא	דָא	דָא
הֶא	הֶא	הֶא	הָא	הָא	הָא
וֹא	וֹא	וֹא	וָא	וַא	וָא
זֹא	זֹא	זֹא	זָא	זָא	זָא
חֹא	חֹא	חֹא	חָא	חָא	חָא

4 Circle the silent Alef.

אַבָּא   בָּא   בָּא

5 Read aloud:

בָּה	בָּה	בָּה	בְּ	בְּ	בְּ
גָה	גָה	גָה	גְ	גְ	גְ
דֶה	דֶה	דֶה	דְ	דְ	דְ

Do you hear the ה in these sounds? The answer is NO.

The ה is silent; it is not heard.

49

6 You know all the letters in this word הַגָּדַּן

Trace with a colored pencil or pen the silent ה.

Trace, with another color, the ה that is heard.

> The letter ה is silent when it has no vowel
> The letter ה is heard when it has a vowel

7 Is the letter ה in the word חַלָה heard or silent?

It is _____.

8 Do you remember these words?

יֶלֶד   בָּא
יַלְדָה   בָּאָה

Fill in the correct word.

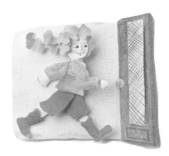

_____ יַלְדָה

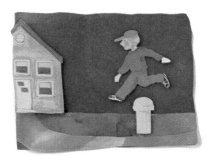

יֶלֶד _____

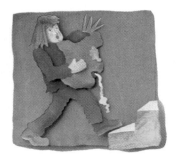

_____ יַלְדָה

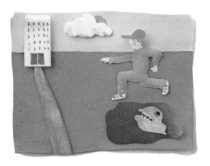

יֶלֶד _____

50

1 Here is one way of writing numbers:

    1   2   3   4   5   6   7   8

Here is another way of writing numbers:

    I   II   III   IV   V   VI   VII   VIII

There is a third way of writing numbers, using the Alef-Bet.

5 = ה	1 = א
—— = ו	2 = ב
—— = ז	—— = ג
8 = ח	4 = ד

2 Do arithmetic with Hebrew letters.

ו	ה	ד	ג	א	א
+	+	+	+	+	+
			ד	ג	ב
———	———	———	———	———	———
ה	ה	ה			ז

ה	ה	ה	ה	ה	ה
—	—	—	—	—	—
	א		ה	ג	ב
———	———	———	———	———	———
ד	א				

51

1 Play Alef-Bet relays.

Divide into two, three, or four groups of equal size.

When the signal is given, the first member of each group should write the letter א on the blackboard and then pass the chalk to the second member of the group.

The second member should write the letter ב on the board and then pass the chalk to the third member.

Each time, the person with the chalk should write the next letter of the Alef-Bet and pass on the chalk.

Which group will be the first to complete the letters from א to ת?

---

2 Make a Bingo card with the Alef-Bet.

At the end of this book, you will find Hebrew sounds arranged in squares. Cut out each of the squares and mix them well.

Now choose any 24 of the cut-outs and arrange and glue them on a card to play the Bingo game.

The 24 cut-outs you choose will probably be different from the 24 that others will choose. So there will be different Bingo cards in the class.

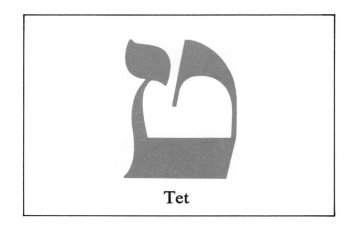

Tet

1 This is the ninth letter of the Alef-Bet   ט

It is called Tet   ט

It has the sound of T as in Talit and Mazal Tov.

2 Circle the letter Tet: מַזָּל טוֹב   יוֹם טוֹב   טוֹב   טַלִית

3 The letter ט is written this way:

first this

then this

Practice writing the whole ט.

___ ___ ___ ___ ___ ___ ___

___ ___ ___ ___ ___ ___ ___

4 Read aloud:

טָ	טָא	טָא		טַ	טֵ	טִ
טוֹב	טָא	טָא		טֵ	טֵ	טֵ
חָטָא	חָטָא	חָטָא		טַ	טֶ	טוֹ

זְטָ	טָז	טָן		טוֹ	טִ	טוֹ
טוֹבָה	טוֹבָה	טוֹבָה		טָה	טִי	טָה
אֶטוֹ	אֶטֹ	אוֹטוֹ		טֶה	טֶה	טֶה

53

יוֹם טוֹב	מַזָּל טוֹב
Yom Tov	Mazal Tov

מַזָּל טוֹב Mazal Tov means good luck or congratulations.
מַזָּל means luck and טוֹב means good.

1 Read aloud:

חַג טוֹב	אַבָּא טוֹב	מַזָּל טוֹב
יֶלֶד טוֹב	דָג טוֹב	יֶלֶד טוֹב

2 יוֹם טוֹב is read Yom Tov; יוֹם means day; טוֹב means good.

יוֹם טוֹב means Good Day.

יוֹם טוֹב may also have a special meaning. It may mean חַג holiday.

You may have heard people say in the synagogue:

"Have a good יוֹם טוֹב"

3 Write טוֹב for the picture describing something which is good.

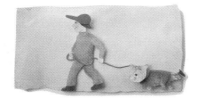

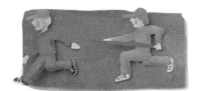

_____

_____

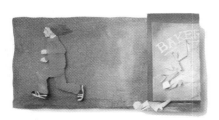

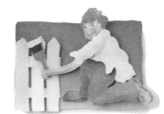

_____

_____

4 Fill in the correct word.

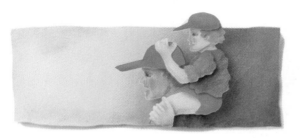

טוֹב _____

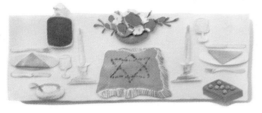

יוֹם _____

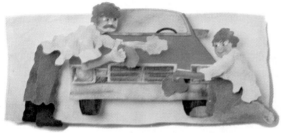

יֶלֶד _____

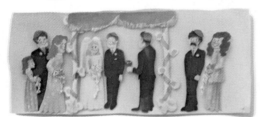

מַזָּל _____

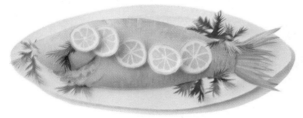

טוֹב _____

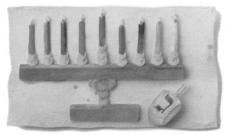

טוֹב _____

חַג	אַבָּא	דָּג	טוֹב

55

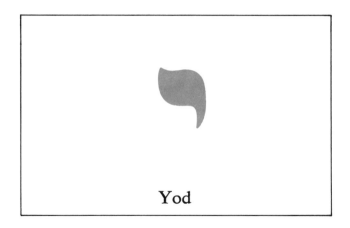

Yod

1 This is the tenth letter of the Alef-Bet ◌

It is called Yod ◌

It has the sound of Y as in You and the Hebrew word Yom.

◌ is the smallest letter of the Alef-Bet.

2 Practice writing the ◌

____ ____ ____ ____ ____

____ ____ ____ ____ ____

3 Circle the letter Yod.

יֶלֶד   יַלְדָה   יְלָדִים   בָּאִים   יוֹם טוֹב

4 ◌ with ◌ is יָ; ◌ with ◌ is יַ. Both have the sound of Yah.

◌ with ◌ is יֶ; ◌ with ◌ is __. Both have the sound Yeh.

◌ with וֹ is __; ◌ with ◌ is יֹ. Both have the sound Yoh.

◌ with וּ is יוּ; ◌ with ◌ is __. Both have the sound of Yuh.

5 Read aloud:

חִיָה	טִיָה	טִיָה		◌	יִ	יֵ
יוֹדָא	יְדָא	יְדָה		הַיָה	הֵיָה	הָיָה
יְזֶה	יִן	יְזָה		דִיָה	דָיָה	אַיָה

56

6 יוֹם (*yom*) means day.

Here is one way of naming the days of the week:

יוֹם א   יוֹם ___

יוֹם ב   יוֹם ___

יוֹם ג   יוֹם ו

We do not use יוֹם ז because the seventh day of the week has a special name, Shabbat.

What day is today?   יוֹם ___

What day was yesterday?   יוֹם ___

What day will it be tomorrow?   יוֹם ___

On what day of the week were you born?   יוֹם ___

7 The ark is that place in the synagogue in which the Torah is kept.

A beautiful curtain usually hangs over the ark.

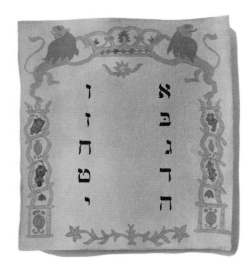

Look at the picture. Why is the curtain in this picture decorated with the first ten letters of the Alef-Bet? _____

_____

_____

The Vowel	The Vowel
_____ ●	_____ ●
Chirik without the Yod	Chirik with the Yod

1 Here is a new pair of vowels:

Chirik with Yod as in וִי הִי דִי גִי בִּי אִי

Chirik without Yod as in וִ הִ דִ גִּ בִּ אִ

They have the sound ee as in Seed and Bee.

2 Circle the Chirik with the Yod.

בָּאִים   יְלָדִים   הַמּוֹצִיא

Circle the Chirik without the Yod.

בָּאִים   דָּוִד   יְלָדִים

3 Practice writing the Chirik with the Yod.

דִ   בִּ   ____ ____ ____ ____ ____

Practice writing the Chirik without the Yod.

____ ____ ____ ____ ____ בִּ

4 Read aloud:

אִיאוֹ	אִיאוֹ		אִי	אִי	אִי
בָּבָא	בְּבָה		בִּ	בִּ	בִּ
דּוֹנִי	גֵּגִי		גִי	גִ	גִי
זוֹהִי	בּוֹאִי		דָּדִי	הַהִי	גִּגִי
הַבִּיטִי	טוֹבִי		זִינָה	דּוֹדִי	חִטָּה

58

1   Now you know the first ten letters of the Alef-Bet.

וַיֵּלֶד וְיַלְדָּה	ו	אַבָּא	א
מְזוּזָה מַזָּל טוֹב	ז	בָּא בָּאָה בָּאִים	ב
חַג חַלָּה חֶדֶר	ח	גָּדוֹל	ג
טוֹב	ט	דָּג	ד
יוֹם יוֹם טוֹב יוֹם א	י	הַגָּדָה	ה

2   Circle the words which describe things that you can touch.

חַלָּה   אַבָּא   בָּא   דָּג   טוֹב

הַגָּדָה   יוֹם   חַג   יֶלֶד   יַלְדָּה

3   Circle the word which describes the picture.

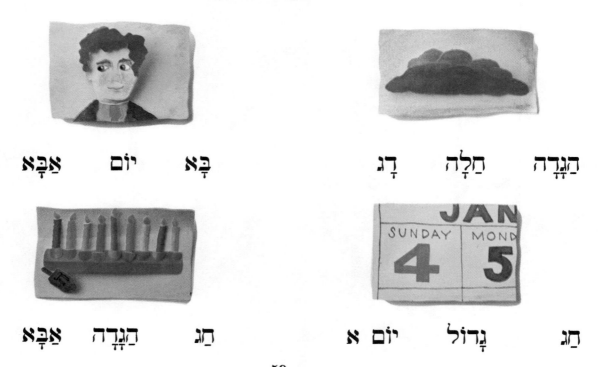

בָּא   יוֹם   אַבָּא

הַגָּדָה   חַלָּה   דָּג

חַג   הַגָּדָה   אַבָּא

גָּדוֹל   יוֹם א   חַג

59

4 You now know five pairs of vowels:

Kamats ָ and Patach ַ as in אָ and אַ

Tserei ֵ and Segol ֶ as in בֵּ and בֶּ

Cholam with Vav וֹ and Cholam without Vav ֹ as in אוֹ and אֹ

Shuruk וּ and Kubuts ֻ as in אוּ and אֻ

Chirik with Yod ִי and Chirik without Yod ִ as in אִי and אִ

5 Read aloud:

טוֹ טוֹא טֹא	חִי הִי הִי	אַ אָ אֵ אִ
יוֹ יְ יוֹ	וִי נְ וִי	בֶּ בֵּ בְּ
יוּטָא יוּבָא	זֶה זֶה זָה	גוֹ גְ גַ
דְּבָה דַּגָה	חָא חֶא חֵא	דוּ דְּ דוּ

6 Arithmetic with Hebrew letters.

9 = ט	5 = ה	1 = א
___ = י	___ = ו	2 = ב
11 = יא	7 = ז	___ = ג
___ = יב	___ = ח	4 = ד

7 What time is it?

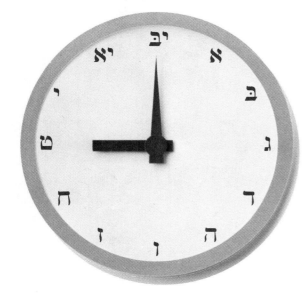

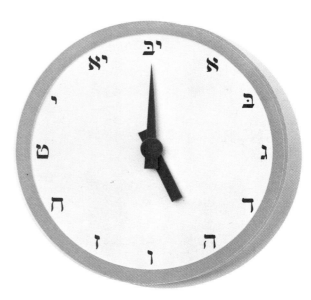

The time is _____   The time is _____

60

A Jewish legend says that the Ten Commandments were written by God on two tablets.

When Moses came down from Mount Sinai and saw the Israelites worshiping the golden calf, he became angry and threw the Tablets to the ground.

As the Tablets were shattered to pieces, the first ten letters

י   ט   ח   ז   ו   ה   ד   ג   ב   א

rose up and flew toward heaven.

And after them flew all the other letters of the Alef-Bet.

מַזָּל טוֹב

Mazal Tov

On the next page you will find a game.

1. The winner is the player who first reaches the מַזָּל טוֹב square.
2. The first player rolls the dice. If the dice show number 4, for example, the player puts a small card on the fourth square, which is אַ
3. The second player rolls the dice. If the dice show 5, the player puts the card on the fifth square which is אוֹ
4. Move from right to left on the א row, from left to right on the ב row, and so on.
5. The arrows help the player skip upward or downward.

Boxes without sounds are also to be played.

We wish you מַזָּל טוֹב *Mazal Tov.*

61

מַזָל טוֹב

מַזָל טוֹב	זֶה	זֶ	זֵ	זִ	זִי	זֻ	זוּ	זֹ	זוֹ	זַ	זָ
	וֶ	וֵ	וֻ	ווּ	וִ	וִי	וֹ	ווֹ	וָ	וָ	
הָא	הִ	הִי	הֻ	הוּ	הֶ	הֵ	הֹ	הוֹ	הַ	הָ	
	דָא	דִ	דִי	דֻ	דוּ	דֹ	דוֹ	דֶ	דֵ	דַ	דָ
גָה	גִ	גִי	גֻ	גוּ	גֹ	גוֹ	גֶ	גֵ	גַ	גָ	
בָּה	בָּא	בִּ	בִּי	בֻּ	בּוּ	בֹּ	בּוֹ	בֶּ	בֵּ	בַּ	בָּ
		אִ	אִי	אֻ	אוּ	אֹ	אוֹ	אֶ	אֵ	אַ	אָ

Start here

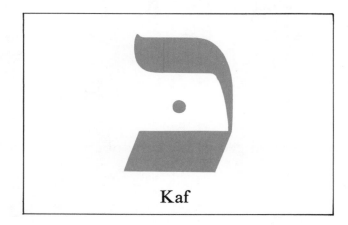

Kaf

1 This is the letter Kaf ‎כ

It has the sound of K as in Yom Kippur and Sukot.

2 Circle the letter Kaf: ‎חֲנֻכָּה ‎ ‎סֻכָּה ‎ ‎יוֹם כִּפּוּר

3 The letter ‎כ, like many other Hebrew letters, is a picture of a word. The word Kaf means the "palm of the hand."

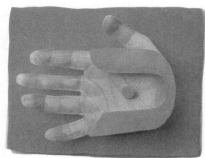

4 Practice writing the ‎כ.

_____ _____ _____ ⠃ ⡃

_____ _____ _____ _____ _____

5 How does ‎כ sound with the vowels you know?

‎כ with ‎ָ is ‎כָּ; ‎כ with ‎ַ is _____

‎כ with ‎ֶ is ‎כֶּ; ‎כ with ‎ֵ is _____

‎כ with ‎וֹ is ‎כוֹ; ‎כ with ‎ִ is _____

‎כ with ‎וּ is ‎כוּ; ‎כ with ‎ְ is _____

‎כ with ‎ִי is ‎כִּי; ‎כ with ‎ֲ is _____

63

6 Check those groups where all the sounds are the same.

בְּכָה בְּכָה בְּכָה בְּכָה ☐	כָּא כָּא כָּא כָּא ☐	כִּ כִּי כִּי ☐
גְּכָה גְּכָה גְּכָה גְּכָה ☐	כְּ כְּ כְּ כְּ ☐	כֹּו כֹּו כֹּו ☐
זְכָה זְכָה זְכָה זְכָה ☐	כֹ כֹ כֹ כֹ ☐	כָּה כָּה כָּה ☐
טְכִי טְכִי טְכִי טְכִי ☐	כֹּו כֹּו כֹּו כֹּו ☐	כֵּ כֵּ כֵּ ☐

7 Check the line which is arranged in correct alphabetical order.

י	כ	ט	ח	ז	ו	ה	ד	ג	ב	אָ ☐
כֵּ	יֵ	טֶ	חֶ	זֶ	וֵ	הֵ	דֵ	גֵ	בֵּ	אֵ ☐
כֵ	יֶ	טֶ	חֶ	זֶ	וֶ	הֶ	דֶ	גֶ	בֶ	אֶ ☐

8 The letter כ appears in the name of three Jewish holidays.

Sukot חַג הַסֻּכּוֹת   Yom Kippur יוֹם כִּפּוּר

Chanukah חַג הַחֲנֻכָּה

Circle the name of the holiday which describes the picture.

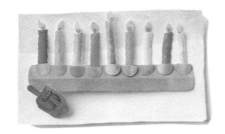

יוֹם כִּפּוּר
חַג הַחֲנֻכָּה
חַג הַסֻּכּוֹת

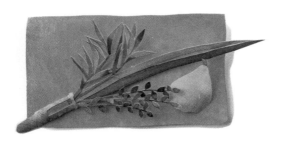

יוֹם כִּפּוּר
חַג הַחֲנֻכָּה
חַג הַסֻּכּוֹת

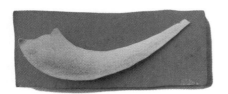

חַג הַסֻּכּוֹת
חַג הַחֲנֻכָּה
יוֹם כִּפּוּר

1   Learn these words.

who (*mi*)   מִי   mother (*ima*)   אִמָּא

2   Check the correct answer.

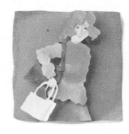

☐ יְלָדִים בָּאִים   ☐ אַבָּא בָּא
☐ יֶלֶד וְיַלְדָּה בָּאִים   ☐ אִמָּא בָּאָה

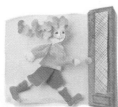

☐ אִמָּא בָּאָה   ☐ אַבָּא וְאִמָּא בָּאִים
☐ יַלְדָּה בָּאָה   ☐ אַבָּא וְיַלְדָּה בָּאִים

מִי גָּדוֹל ?
Who Is Big?

3   Check the correct answer.

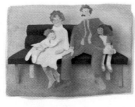

☐ יַלְדָּה   ☐ יֶלֶד
☐ אִמָּא   ☐ אַבָּא

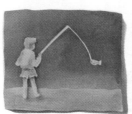

☐ יֶלֶד   ☐ דָּג
☐ אִמָּא   ☐ אַבָּא

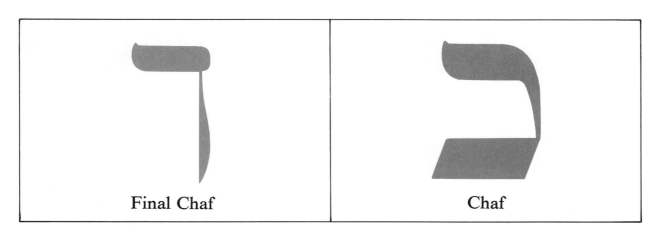

| Final Chaf | Chaf |

1 This is the letter Chaf כ

It is like the letter כּ but without the dot in the middle.

The letter Chaf is a sister of Kaf: כ כּ

It has a sound similar to the Hebrew letter ח.

2 Circle the letter Chaf: בְּרָכוֹת   בְּרָכָה   סֻכּוֹת   כִּפּוּר   יוֹם

3 Read aloud:

כָּכָה	כָּכָה	כָּכָה	כָּכָה		הָכִי	הָכִי	הָכִי
זָכָה	זָכָה	זָכָה			בּוֹכֶה	בּוֹכֶה	בּוֹכֶה
בָּכוּ	בָּכוּ	בָּכוּ			בְּכִי	בְּכִי	בְּכִי

4 This is the final letter Chaf ךְ

The final letter ךְ has the sound of the כ, but it is written *only* at the *end* of a word.

Circle the final letter Chaf: בְּרָכָה   בָּרוּךְ   מֶלֶךְ   יוֹם כִּפּוּר

5 Practice writing the ךְ.

6 Here are the sister letters you already know:

| Bet | בּ | | Kaf | כּ |
| Vet | ב | | Chaf | כ |

66

7 The word for blessings in Hebrew is בְּרָכוֹת. It is pronounced *Berachot*. A single blessing is בְּרָכָה. It is pronounced *Berachah*.

The בְּרָכוֹת are a way of giving thanks to God for many things. Best known are the בְּרָכוֹת we say when we eat, drink, and light candles for the Shabbat or holidays.

When we eat bread, we cut a slice of the bread and then recite the בְּרָכָה called *Hamotzi*, a word which means "bring out."

The הַמּוֹצִיא blessing is recited by everyone at the table.

Baruch Atah	בָּרוּךְ אַתָּה
Adonai Elohenu	אֲדֹנָי אֱלֹהֵינוּ
Melech ha'olam	מֶלֶךְ הָעוֹלָם
Hamotzi lechem	הַמּוֹצִיא לֶחֶם
Min ha'aretz	מִן הָאָרֶץ

Blessed is
The Lord our God
Ruler of the universe
Who causes bread to come
From the earth

We praise God for causing bread to come from the earth.

Hamotzi lechem	הַמּוֹצִיא לֶחֶם
Min ha'aretz	מִן הָאָרֶץ

67

Hamotzi is perhaps the best-known בְּרָכָה since we eat bread at most meals.

Even on Shabbat when we eat chalah instead of regular bread, we recite the בְּרָכָה *Hamotzi Lechem*.

The Shabbat meal begins when אַבָּא or אִמָּא uncovers the חַלָה, cuts a slice, and recites:

Baruch Atah	בָּרוּךְ אַתָּה
Adonai Elohenu	אֲדֹנָי אֱלֹהֵינוּ
Melech ha'olam	מֶלֶךְ הָעוֹלָם
Hamotzi lechem	הַמּוֹצִיא לֶחֶם
Min ha'aretz	מִן הָאָרֶץ

Blessed is
The Lord our God
Ruler of the universe
Who causes bread to come
From the earth

Even on Pesach when we eat matzah and not bread, we recite הַמּוֹצִיא and thank God.

הַמּוֹצִיא לֶחֶם מִן הָאָרֶץ

8	בָּרוּךְ	יוֹם טוֹב	טוֹב	יוֹם כִּפּוּר	בְּרָכוֹת	בְּרָכָה

How many times does the letter בּ appear in the above words? _____ times

How many times does the letter ב appear in the above words? _____ times

How many times does the letter כּ appear in the above words? _____ times

How many times does the letter כ appear in the above words? _____ times

How many times does the letter ךְ appear in the above words? _____ times

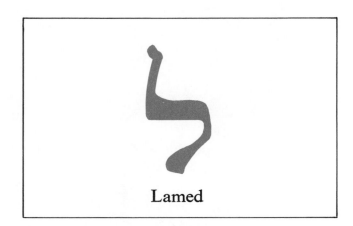

Lamed

1 This is the letter Lamed ל

It has the sound of L as in Chalah.

2 Circle the letter Lamed.

מֶלֶךְ יְלָדִים יַלְדָה יֶלֶד לֶחֶם חַלָה

3 The letter ל is written this way:

first this ⤸

then this ⟋

Practice writing ל.

___ ___ ___ ___ ⟋ ⟋

4 In each group, circle the sound which is different from the others.

לָה	לֹא	לֹא	טַלְיָה	טָלֶה	טָלֶה	לְ	לְ	לְ	לָ
לִי	לָה	לִי	דְלִי	דְלִי	דְלִי	לִי	לְ	לֻ	לְ
לֻ	לֹו	לֻ	לֵאָה	לוּאָה	לֵאָה	לִי	לֻ	לִי	לִי

5 Read aloud the sounds in Exercise 4.

6 Circle the words which describe things you can touch.

חַג	בָּא	מְזוּזָה	לֶחֶם	בְּרָכָה	חַלָה	דָג
אִמָא	טוֹב	מַזָל	אַבָּא	יוֹם	גָדוֹל	הַגָדָה
מִי	בְּרָכוֹת	לֶחֶם	טוֹב	יוֹם	יַלְדָה	יֶלֶד

69

The Hebrew Calendar

Two thousand years ago the Jewish people did not have a written calendar. Each month began with the new moon.

On the last day of the month, the people in Jerusalem would watch for the appearance of the new moon. That night, bonfires would be lit on the mountains surrounding the city. These were signals to other villages that the new moon was seen.

The following day was the celebration of Rosh Chodesh which means the first day of the new month.

Having no written calendar was difficult, especially for Jews in faraway countries. They were always afraid that the message about the new month would reach them too late. Therefore, in those days, they decided to observe two days of Rosh Chodesh instead of one.

They also began to celebrate two days at the beginning of important holidays such as Sukot or Pesach. In this way they were sure that one of the two days was the correct one.

Today, we can look at a Hebrew calendar and know when a holiday or Rosh Chodesh begins.

The calendar has 12 months, and each month has a Hebrew name.

Some months have 30 days, and others have only 29 days.

One way in which the Alef-Bet is used as numerals, even today, is in the Hebrew calendar. Here is an example:

יוֹם שַׁבָּת	יוֹם ו	יוֹם ה	יוֹם ד	יוֹם ג	יוֹם ב	יוֹם א
ו	ה	ד	ג	ב	א	
יג	יב	יא	י	ט	ח	ז
כ	יט	יח	יז	טז	טו	יד
כז	כו	כה	כד	כג	כב	כא
				ל	כט	כח

1 Notice that the days of the week are written at the top of this calendar.

Thursday _____ יוֹם   Sunday   יוֹם א

Friday _____ יוֹם   _____ יוֹם ב

Shabbat   יוֹם שַׁבָּת   _____ יוֹם ג

            _____ יוֹם ד

2 Look at a Jewish calendar and find the name of the present month.

_____

3 How many days are there in this month? _____

4 Are there any Jewish holidays this month? _____
What are they? _____ _____ _____

5 What else does the calendar tell you about this month? _____

_____

_____

_____

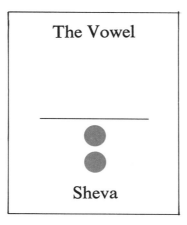

The Vowel

Sheva

1   Here are the five pairs of vowels you already know:

Kamats ָ and Patach ַ as in אָ and אַ

Tserei ֵ and Segol ֶ as in אֵ and אֶ

Cholam with Vav וֹ and without Vav ֹ as in אוֹ and אֹ

Kubutz ֻ and Shuruk וּ as in אוּ and אֻ

Chirik with Yod ִי and without Yod ִ as in אִי and אִ

2   Here is a new vowel. It is called Sheva   ְ

Circle the vowel Sheva.

יַלְדָה   וְאַבָּא   בְּרָכוֹת   בְּרָכָה

3   The vowel ְ allows the letter under which it appears to sound itself. It has the sound of B in Bread, the sound Sh in *Shema*, or the sound of M in Mezuzah.

Sound out these letters with the vowel ְ

לְ   כְּ   יְ   טְ   חְ   זְ   וְ

4   Read aloud:

יַלְדָה   יֶלֶד וְיַלְדָה   אַבָּא וְאִמָּא

72

5 Read these words:

בָּרוּךְ   חַג   גָּדוֹל

יוֹם טוֹב   חֶדֶר   לֶחֶם

יוֹם   יֶלֶד   מַזָּל טוֹב

> The last letter of these words has no vowel
> It sounds almost as if it had the vowel ְ under it

---

6 Circle the words where the last letter sounds almost as if it had the vowel ְ under it.

חַלָּה   לֶחֶם   יַלְדָּה   חַג

אַבָּא   יוֹם טוֹב   הַגָּדָה

הַבְדָּלָה   יֶלֶד   בָּא   בָּרוּךְ

מַזָּל טוֹב   בְּרָכוֹת   בְּרָכָה

Hidden Words

Look down and across and circle the hidden words.

Down				*Across*
chalah	ר	ד	ח	cheder, room
holiday	ם	ח	ל	bread
	ה	ד	ג	ה	Haggadah

הַגָּדָה	חַלָּה	לֶחֶם	חֶדֶר	חַג

73

מִי לֹא אוֹכֵל ?	מִי אוֹכֵל ?
Who Is Not Eating?	Who Is Eating?

1 Learn these words.

no or not (lo) לֹא   eats, m. (ochel) אוֹכֵל

2

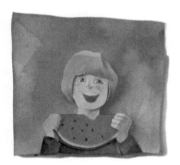

מִי אוֹכֵל ?
☐ אַבָּא אוֹכֵל
☐ יֶלֶד אוֹכֵל
☐ דָּג אוֹכֵל

3

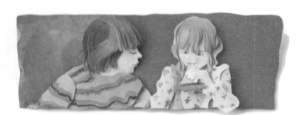

מִי לֹא אוֹכֵל ?
☐ אַבָּא אוֹכֵל
☐ יֶלֶד אוֹכֵל
☐ יֶלֶד לֹא אוֹכֵל

4

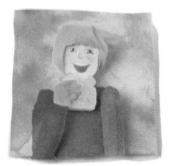

מִי אוֹכֵל לֶחֶם ?
☐ אַבָּא אוֹכֵל דָּג
☐ אַבָּא אוֹכֵל לֶחֶם
☐ יֶלֶד אוֹכֵל לֶחֶם
☐ יֶלֶד לֹא אוֹכֵל

5

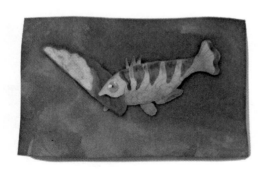

מִי אוֹכֵל חַלָּה ?
☐ יֶלֶד אוֹכֵל דָּג
☐ אַבָּא אוֹכֵל דָּג
☐ דָּג אוֹכֵל חַלָּה
☐ יֶלֶד אוֹכֵל חַלָּה

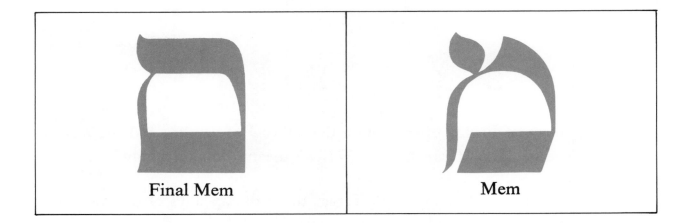

Final Mem	Mem

1 This is the letter Mem   מ

It has the sound of M as in *Hamotzi* or Mezuzah.

2 Circle the letter Mem: הַמּוֹצִיא   מִי   מְזוּזָה   מַזָּל טוֹב   אִמָּא

3 The letter מ is written this way:

first this   ⟁   then this   ⟁

Practice writing the מ.

___   ___   ___   ___   ⟁   ⟁

4 This is the final Mem   ם

It has the sound of the מ but it is written *only* at the *end* of the word.

5 Circle the final Mem: הַמּוֹצִיא   יוֹם   אִמָּא   מִי   לֶחֶם

6 How many times does the מ appear in the above line?   _____ times

How many times does the letter ם appear in the line?   _____ times

7 Practice writing the ם.

___   ___   ___   ___   ⬚   ☐

8 Add the missing letter.

חֶם☐	ם ☐לְ	☐לֶחֶ	לֶחֶם
וֹם☐	ם ☐יֹ	☐יוֹ	יוֹם
מָא☐	א ☐א	☐אִמָּ	אִמָּא

75

Shabbat starts on Friday evening with the lighting of candles and the reciting of the *Kiddush*. The Hebrew word *Kiddush* means "making holy."

Shabbat helps the Jewish people forget the ordinary days of the week with their ordinary activities and, for one day, think and do things that are holy.

Shabbat ends with a special ceremony called *Havdalah*. The word הַבְדָּלָה means "separation." The main words chanted in the *Havdalah*:

. . .*Hamavdil bein kodesh lechol*   ...הַמַבְדִּיל בֵּין קֹדֶשׁ לְחוֹל

. . .Separates the holy from the unholy

The *Kiddush* is a way of saying that the regular weekdays stop and a holy day of prayer and rest begins.

The הַבְדָּלָה is a way of saying that the holy day has come to an end and the regular days of the week begin.

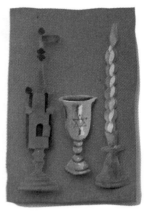

Ask your teacher, your cantor, or your rabbi to recite the הַבְדָּלָה ceremony. You will need a *Havdalah* candle, wine, spices, and a special spice box.

Find the הַבְדָּלָה ceremony in the prayer book. It has a beautiful melody. Look for the words:
Hamavdil bein kodesh lechol   הַמַבְדִּיל בֵּין קֹדֶשׁ לְחוֹל

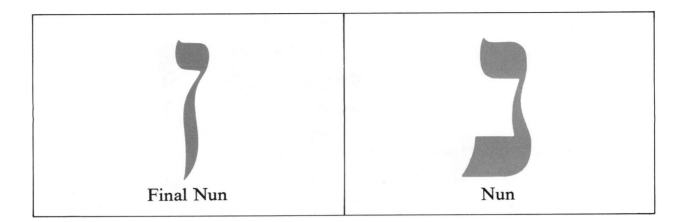

| Final Nun | Nun |

1 This is the letter Nun נ

It has the sound of N as in No or Chanukah.

2 Circle the letter Nun: אֲנִי נֵר חֲנֻכִּיָה חֲנֻכָּה

3 Practice writing the נ.

___ ___ ___ ___ ⁞ ⨼

4 This is the final Nun ן

The final Nun has the sound of the נ, but it is written *only* at the *end* of the word.

5 Circle the final Nun.

מִנְיָן נֵר גֶּפֶן קָטָן חֲנֻכִּיָה חֲנֻכָּה אָמֵן

How many times did the letter Nun appear in the above line? _____ times

How many times did the final Nun appear in the above line? _____ times

6 Practice writing the ן.

___ ___ ___ ___ ⟊ ⟊

7 Here are the final letters which you already know:

ן   ם   ך

8   Match.

Final Mem	ן	Nun	מ	ן	מ
Final Nun	ם	Mem	ל	ם	כ
Final Chaf	ך	Lamed	נ	ך	נ

9   Do you remember these words?

no	לֹא	boy	יֶלֶד	and	וְ	father	אַבָּא
bread	לֶחֶם	girl	יַלְדָּה	holiday	חַג	eats, m.	אוֹכֵל
				chalah	חַלָה	mother	אִמָּא

10   Learn these new words.

children (*yeladim*)	יְלָדִים	eat, pl. (*ochelim*)	אוֹכְלִים
what (*mah*)	מֶה	I (*ani*)	אֲנִי
candle (*ner*)	נֵר	Chanukah (*Chanukah*)	חֲנֻכָּה
		Chanukiah (*Chanukiah*)	חֲנֻכִּיָה

11   Match words and pictures.

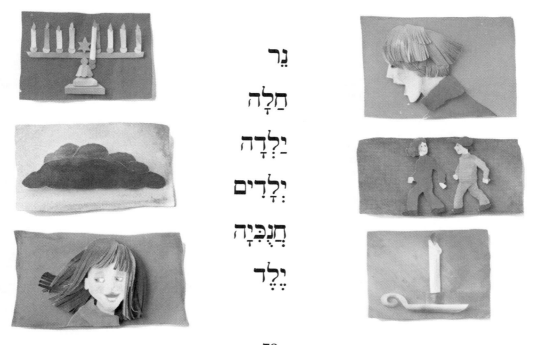

נֵר

חַלָה

יַלְדָּה

יְלָדִים

חֲנֻכִּיָה

יֶלֶד

12 Circle the correct answers.

מָה אוֹכְלִים ? — לֶחֶם נֵר חַלָה חַג חֲנֻכִּיָה

מָה לֹא אוֹכְלִים ? — לֶחֶם נֵר חַלָה חַג חֲנֻכִּיָה

13 Each of the people below is saying something. Find the sentence which is correct for each picture and write it in.

אֲנִי יֶלֶד   אֲנִי אַבָּא

אֲנִי יַלְדָה   אֲנִי אִמָא

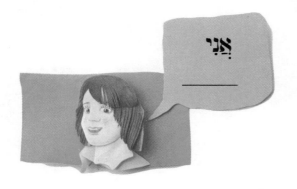
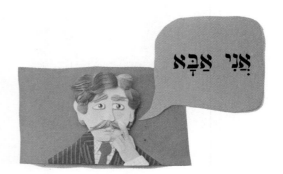

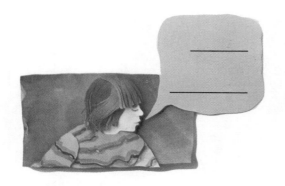
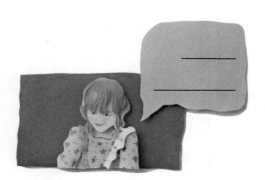

14 Do you know your Hebrew name?

Write it here: אֲנִי _____

79

15 Check the sentence which describes the picture.

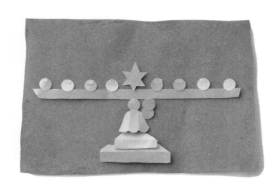

☐ חַג הַחֲנֻכָּה
☐ לֶחֶם וְחַלָּה
☐ יֶלֶד וְיַלְדָּה
☐ אַבָּא וְאִמָּא

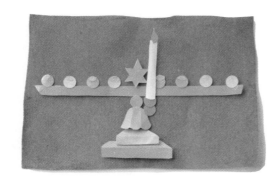

☐ חֲנֻכִּיָּה וְחַלָּה
☐ חֲנֻכִּיָּה וְנֵר
☐ יֶלֶד וַחֲנֻכִּיָּה
☐ יֶלֶד וְנֵר

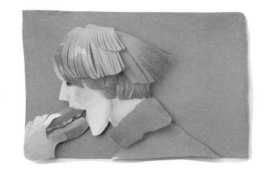

☐ אַבָּא וְאִמָּא
☐ נֵר חֲנֻכָּה
☐ אֲנִי אַבָּא
☐ יֶלֶד אוֹכֵל

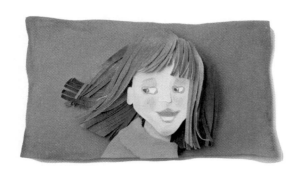

☐ אֲנִי יַלְדָּה
☐ אֲנִי אַבָּא
☐ אֲנִי אוֹכֵל לֶחֶם
☐ חַג הַחֲנֻכָּה

80

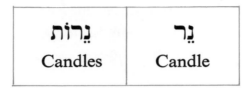

נֵרוֹת	נֵר
Candles	Candle

The Hebrew word for candle is נֵר *ner*. The word for more than one candle is
נֵרוֹת *nerot*.

We light נֵרוֹת to bring in the Shabbat and to end the Shabbat.

On Friday night as the sun sets, we light the נֵרוֹת and recite the בְּרָכָה:

Baruch Atah	בָּרוּךְ אַתָּה
Adonai Elohenu	אֲדֹנָי אֱלֹהֵינוּ
Melech ha'olam	מֶלֶךְ הָעוֹלָם
Asher kideshanu bemitzvotav	אֲשֶׁר קִדְּשָׁנוּ בְּמִצְוֺתָיו
Vetsivanu lehadlik	וְצִוָּנוּ לְהַדְלִיק
Ner shel Shabbat	נֵר שֶׁל שַׁבָּת

Blessed is
The Lord our God
Ruler of the universe
Who makes us holy with His mitzvot
And commands us to kindle
The lights of Shabbat

It is usually the woman who lights the נֵרוֹת and recites the בְּרָכָה, but men
may also light the Shabbat candles.

When any בְּרָכָה is recited, it is customary to say אָמֵן. Amen means
"let it be." By saying אָמֵן we participate in the prayer. We wish אָמֵן let it
be....

אָמֵן is a Hebrew word which is more than two thousand years old.

81

It is the custom to light נֵרוֹת, not only on Friday evenings and Shabbat night, but also on holidays. In fact, one holiday, חַג הַחֲנֻכָּה, is called the Festival of Lights. On חֲנֻכָּה we light a special menorah called חֲנֻכִּיָּה.

Look at a חֲנֻכִּיָּה.

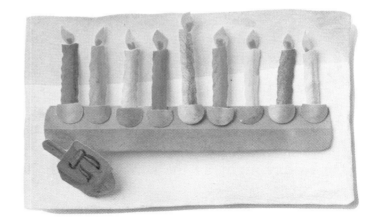

How many places for candles do you see? _____

Why do we light the חֲנֻכִּיָּה? _____

_____

_____

When the Chanukah candles נֵרוֹת חֲנֻכָּה are lit, the custom is to recite a בְּרָכָה:

Baruch Atah	בָּרוּךְ אַתָּה
Adonai Elohenu	אֲדֹנָי אֱלֹהֵינוּ
Melech ha'olam	מֶלֶךְ הָעוֹלָם
Asher kideshanu bemitzvotav	אֲשֶׁר קִדְּשָׁנוּ בְּמִצְוֹתָיו
Vetsivanu lehadlik	וְצִוָּנוּ לְהַדְלִיק
Ner shel Chanukah	נֵר שֶׁל חֲנֻכָּה

    Blessed is
    The Lord our God
    Ruler of the universe
    Who makes us holy with His mitzvot
    And commands us to kindle
    The lights of Chanukah

1 Compare the בְּרָכָה made over the Shabbat candles with the בְּרָכָה made over נֵרוֹת חֲנֻכָּה.

א) בָּרוּךְ אַתָּה, אֲדֹנָי אֱלֹהֵינוּ, מֶלֶךְ הָעוֹלָם
אֲשֶׁר קִדְּשָׁנוּ בְּמִצְוֹתָיו
וְצִוָּנוּ לְהַדְלִיק נֵר שֶׁל שַׁבָּת

ב) בָּרוּךְ אַתָּה, אֲדֹנָי אֱלֹהֵינוּ, מֶלֶךְ הָעוֹלָם
אֲשֶׁר קִדְּשָׁנוּ בְּמִצְוֹתָיו
וְצִוָּנוּ לְהַדְלִיק נֵר שֶׁל חֲנֻכָּה

How are the two בְּרָכוֹת different? _____

_____

_____

2 Check the sentences which are parts of blessings.

☐ בָּרוּךְ אַתָּה אֲדֹנָי אֱלֹהֵינוּ
☐ אַבָּא בָּא
☐ מֶלֶךְ הָעוֹלָם
☐ יַלְדָּה בָּאָה
☐ נֵר שֶׁל חֲנֻכָּה
☐ אַבָּא וְאִמָּא בָּאִים
☐ הַמּוֹצִיא לֶחֶם מִן הָאָרֶץ

83

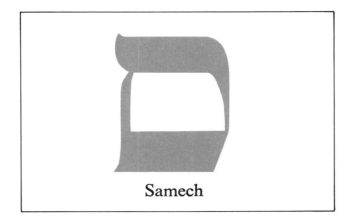

Samech

1 This is the letter Samech   ס

It has the sound of S as in Sukot or Sukah.

2 Circle the letter Samech.

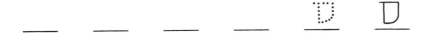

כְּנֶסֶת   בֵּית   סִדוּר   סֶדֶר   פֶּסַח   סֻכָּה   סֻכּוֹת

3 Practice writing the   ס.

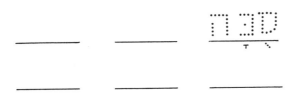

____   ____   ____   ____

4 Write the word   סֻכָּה

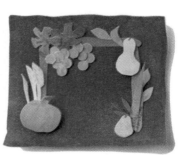

_____   _____

_____   _____   _____

5 Now write the ס with different vowels to give as many different sounds as you can.

____   ____   ____   ____

84

6 In each group, circle the sound which is different from the others.

סָ סָ סָ | סוּ סֹ סֹ | סֹ סֹ סֻ

סָ סָ סָ | סָ סָ סָ | סֶ סָ סָ

סָ סֻ סָ | סִ סֹ סֻ | סִ סֹ סִ

סֹ סוּ סָ | סֻ סָ סָ | ס סָ סָ

סֻכָּה סֻכָּה סֻכָּה סֻכָּה סְכָכָה

זֻכֶּה סֻכָּה סֻכָּה

טֻים טַיִם טַיִם טום

סָבִיב סְבִיבוֹן סְבִיבוֹן

7 Read aloud:

סָ סָ סָ | אוֹ אוֹ אוֹ | אוֹ אוֹ אוֹ

כָּה כָּה כָּה | כֵּלִים כֵּלִים כֵּלִים | כָּל כָּל כָּל

סֻכָּה סֻכָּה סֻכָּה | אוֹכְלִים אוֹכְלִים אוֹכְלִים | אוֹכֵל אוֹכֵל אוֹכֵל

8 Fill in the missing part of the word.

___כֵּל | אוֹ___ | אוֹכֵל

___כֵּלִים | אוֹ___ | אוֹכְלִים

___כָּה | ___סָ | סֻכָּה

9 Match.

Vav	ד	Alef	א
Dalet	ו	Bet	ג
Hei	ה	Gimel	ב

Nun	מ	Lamed	י	Tet	ז
Mem	נ	Yod	כ	Zayin	ח
Samech	ס	Kaf	ל	Chet	ט

85

סֻכּוֹת

Sukot

The Sukot holiday, חַג הַסֻּכּוֹת, is important for many reasons.

חַג הַסֻּכּוֹת is a harvest holiday. Many years ago, farmers used to pick their crops and come to the Temple in Jerusalem. They celebrated, were happy, and gave gifts to the poor.

חַג הַסֻּכּוֹת also reminds us of the Israelites who walked for forty years in the Sinai before reaching the Promised Land.

The custom of building a סֻכָּה reminds us of the booths in which the Israelites lived while they were traveling in the desert.

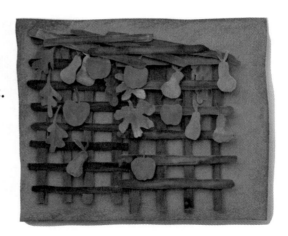

The last day of חַג הַסֻּכּוֹת is called Simchat Torah. It means "the rejoicing of the Torah." On this day, we read the last part of the Torah and start all over again. Our study of Torah never ends.

1 Study these words.

and	וְ	the	הַ	in	בְּ
and mother	וְאִמָּא	the boy	הַיֶּלֶד	sukah	סֻכָּה
and the children	וְהַיְלָדִים	the girl	הַיַּלְדָּה	in the sukah	בַּסֻּכָּה

86

2 Only one sentence is not correct.

Check the sentence which is not correct.

מִי בַּסֻכָּה ?

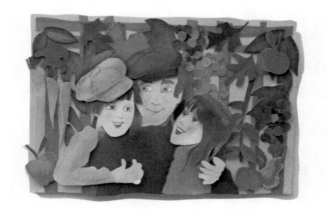

☐ אַבָּא בַּסֻכָּה
☐ יְלָדִים בַּסֻכָּה
☐ אִמָּא בַּסֻכָּה
☐ אַבָּא וְהַיְלָדִים בַּסֻכָּה

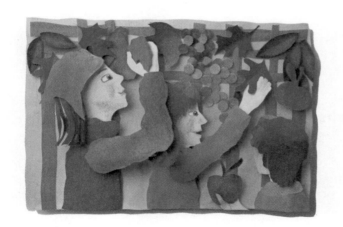

☐ אִמָּא בַּסֻכָּה
☐ יְלָדִים בַּסֻכָּה
☐ יֶלֶד וְיַלְדָּה בַּסֻכָּה
☐ אַבָּא וְאִמָּא בַּסֻכָּה

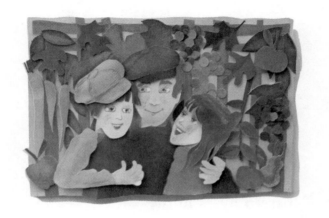

☐ אַבָּא וְהַיֶּלֶד בַּסֻכָּה
☐ אִמָּא וְהַיֶּלֶד בַּסֻכָּה
☐ אַבָּא וְהַיַלְדָּה בַּסֻכָּה
☐ הַיְלָדִים בַּסֻכָּה

Long ago Jews worshiped God by bringing sacrifices. Then things changed and the Jewish people started to worship only through prayer.

The prayers were put into a book called siddur סִדּוּר. Some of the prayers in the siddur are as old as the Bible and some are very new.

Prayer is one of the oldest and most important traditions in Jewish life.

Bring a סִדּוּר to class. In the siddur, find a prayer you already know.

You have already learned several prayers and blessings:

Part of the *Kiddush*, the blessing we recite on the eve of Shabbat and holidays, is on page 26.

Hamotzi, the בְּרָכָה we recite when we eat bread, is on pages 67 and 68.

Havdalah הַבְדָּלָה, the ceremony which says goodbye to the Shabbat, is on page 76.

The בְּרָכָה we say when we light Shabbat candles נֵרוֹת שַׁבָּת is on page 81.

The בְּרָכָה we say when we light Chanukah candles נֵרוֹת חֲנֻכָּה is on page 82.

Ask your teacher to help you find one of these prayers in the סִדּוּר.

טוֹבָה   טוֹב

Good

1   Read aloud:

אַבָּא טוֹב	אִמָּא טוֹבָה	נֵר טוֹב חֲנֻכִּיָּה טוֹבָה
יֶלֶד טוֹב	יַלְדָּה טוֹבָה	מַזָּל טוֹב
לֶחֶם טוֹב	חַלָּה טוֹבָה	יוֹם טוֹב שָׁנָה טוֹבָה
חֶדֶר טוֹב	סֻכָּה טוֹבָה	דָּג טוֹב

2

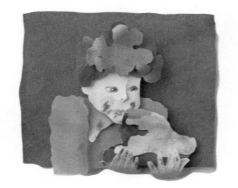

מִי טוֹב ?   מִי טוֹבָה ?

☐ הַיֶּלֶד   ☐ אַבָּא

☐ הַיַּלְדָּה   ☐ אִמָּא

מִי לֹא טוֹב ?   מִי לֹא טוֹבָה ?

☐ הַיַּלְדָּה   ☐ אַבָּא

☐ הַיֶּלֶד   ☐ אִמָּא

3 Fill in the correct word.

בָּא – בָּאָה – בָּאִים   אוֹכֵל – אוֹכֶלֶת – אוֹכְלִים

יֶלֶד בָּא. אַבָּא _____	יֶלֶד אוֹכֵל. אַבָּא _____
יַלְדָה בָּאָה. אִמָּא _____	יַלְדָה אוֹכֶלֶת. אִמָּא _____
יְלָדִים בָּאִים. אַבָּא וְאִמָּא _____	יְלָדִים אוֹכְלִים. אַבָּא וְאִמָּא _____

4 Fill in the correct word.

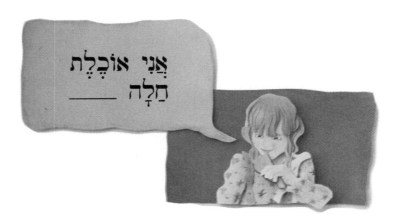

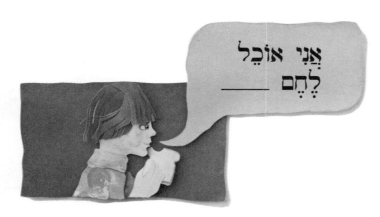

טוֹב	טוֹבָה

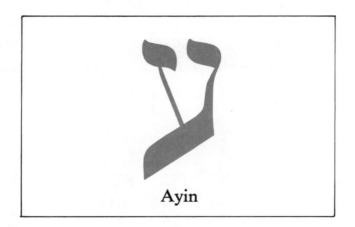

Ayin

1   This is the letter Ayin   עַ

2   Circle the letter Ayin.

עִבְרִית הַשָּׁבוּעוֹת חַג עֲלִיָה שָׁמַע עוֹלָם אָדוֹן

3   The English language does not have the sound of the letter עַ.

     Most Americans find it hard to pronounce the difference between עַ and אַ or עֲ and אֱ.

You will probably sound out עַ as אַ, עֲ as אֱ, עִי as אִי.

4   The letter עַ is written this way:

first this ⌐↓

then this ٱ⌐

Practice writing the עַ.

———   ———   ———   ———   ٱ⌐   ٱ⌐

When the letter **ע** appears at the end of a word
with no vowel under it, the **ע** is almost not heard

5 Read aloud:

בָּא בָּה בָּע | מָא מָה מָע | יָדַע יָדַע יָדַע יָדַע
נָא נָה נָע | זֶע זֶה זֶע | נָגַע נָגַע נָגַע נָגַע

6 Check the line where all the sounds are the same.

☐ חַע זַע זַע | ☐ עֲלָיָה עֲלִי עֲלִי עֲלִי | ☐ עוֹ עוֹ עוֹ ☐
☐ נָע נָע נָע | ☐ עַם עַם עַם עַם | ☐ עוֹלָם עוֹלָם עוֹלָם ☐
☐ עוֹ עוֹ עוֹ | ☐ עֲמִידָה עֲמִי עֲמִי | ☐ אָדוֹן עוֹלָם עֲלָיָה ☐

7 Fill in the missing part of the word.

_____לָם | _____עוֹ | עוֹלָם
_____כֶל | _____וֹ | אוֹכֶל
_____דָה | _____יְלַ | יַלְדָה
_____דִים | _____יְלַ | יְלָדִים

8 Read aloud:

אוֹכֵל — אוֹכֶלֶת — אוֹכְלִים

אַבָּא אוֹכֵל לֶחֶם טוֹב | אִמָּא אוֹכֶלֶת חַלָּה טוֹבָה
אִמָּא אוֹכֶלֶת לֶחֶם טוֹב | אַבָּא אוֹכֵל חַלָּה טוֹבָה
הַיַלְדָה אוֹכֶלֶת לֶחֶם טוֹב | הַיֶּלֶד אוֹכֵל חַלָּה טוֹבָה
הַיְלָדִים אוֹכְלִים לֶחֶם טוֹב | הַיֶּלֶד וְהַיַלְדָה אוֹכְלִים חַלָּה טוֹבָה

עֲלִיָה
Aliyah

In the synagogue, the Torah is read from beginning to end. It takes a whole year to complete the reading. It is read by a person who stands on the pulpit and reads or chants the Torah in Hebrew.

Before each part is read, a member of the congregation comes up to join the reader at the pulpit. This is called an Aliyah עֲלִיָה.

Your first עֲלִיָה to the pulpit is going to be on the day of your Bar Mitzvah or Bat Mitzvah.

The person who is given the honor of an עֲלִיָה has to chant a blessing בְּרָכָה before the part of the Torah is read and a second בְּרָכָה when the reading is finished. Here is part of the first בְּרָכָה:

Baruch Atah	בָּרוּךְ אַתָּה
Adonai Elohenu	אֲדֹנָי אֱלֹהֵינוּ
Melech ha'olam	מֶלֶךְ הָעוֹלָם
Asher bachar banu	אֲשֶׁר בָּחַר בָּנוּ
Mikol ha'amim	מִכָּל הָעַמִּים
Venatan lanu et Torato	וְנָתַן לָנוּ אֶת תּוֹרָתוֹ
Baruch Atah Adonai	בָּרוּךְ אַתָּה אֲדֹנָי
Noten Hatorah	נוֹתֵן הַתּוֹרָה

Blessed is
The Lord our God
Ruler of the universe
Who has chosen us
From all people
By giving us His Torah
Blessed is the Lord
Giver of the Torah

1 Learn to chant the blessing.

Read again this part of the Torah blessing:

Baruch Atah   בָּרוּךְ אַתָּה

Adonai Elohenu   אֲדֹנָי אֱלֹהֵינוּ

Melech ha'olam   מֶלֶךְ הָעוֹלָם

           Blessed is
           The Lord our God
           Ruler of the universe

These six Hebrew words are the beginning of many of the blessings. Do you remember another בְּרָכָה which has the same beginning?

_____

2 God is often called מֶלֶךְ הָעוֹלָם. What does it mean?

_____

3 Make a poster or decorate the words:

אֱלֹהֵינוּ   אֲדֹנָי   אַתָּה   בָּרוּךְ

[blank box]

4 The word עֲלִיָּה has another interesting meaning. It means going to live in Israel. Why do you think going to live in Israel is called עֲלִיָּה?

_____

_____

Crossword Puzzle

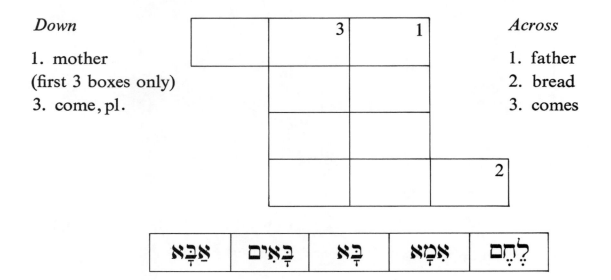

Down

1. mother
(first 3 boxes only)
3. come, pl.

Across

1. father
2. bread
3. comes

אַבָּא   בָּאִים   בָּא   אִמָא   לֶחֶם

Hidden Words

Look down and across and circle the hidden words.

Down

eats

eat, pl.

Across

world

blessing

boy

day

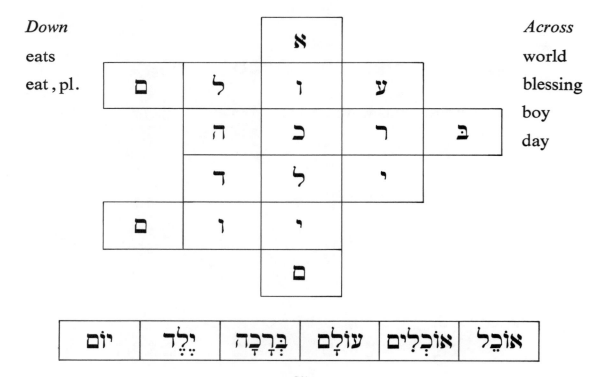

יוֹם   יֶלֶד   בְּרָכָה   עוֹלָם   אוֹכְלִים   אוֹכֵל

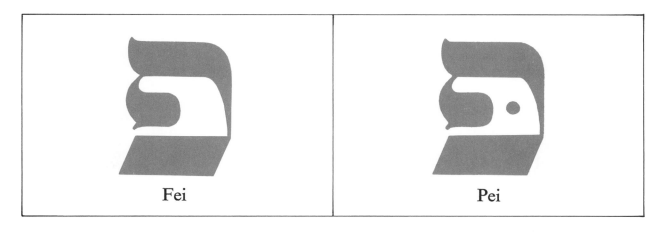

Fei	Pei

1 This is the letter Pei פּ

It has the sound of P as in the holidays Purim, Pesach, and Yom Kippur.

2 Circle the letter Pei.

יוֹם כִּפּוּר   חַג הַפֶּסַח   חַג פּוּרִים   פְּרִי

3 Take out the dot from inside the פּ and you have Fei פ:

Pei פּ   Fei פ

The letter פ has the sound of F as in Flower or the Hebrew Sefer which means book.

4 Circle the letter Pei.

גֶּפֶן   חַג הַפֶּסַח   סֵפֶר   יוֹם כִּפּוּר   אֲפִיקוֹמָן

5 The letter פ is written this way:

first this ⅂↓

then this ⅃

Practice writing the פּ and the פ.

_____ _____ _____ _____ פּ פּ

_____ _____ _____ _____ פ פ

6 Circle the letter Fei.

גֶּפֶן   חַג הַפֶּסַח   סֵפֶר   פּוּרִים   יָפָה

96

7 Read aloud:

<table>
<tr><td>גֶּ גֶּ גֶּ גֶּ</td><td>יָ יָ יָ</td><td>פֶּ פֶּ פֶּ</td></tr>
<tr><td>פֶּן פֶּן פֶּן פֶּן</td><td>פָ פָ פָ</td><td>סַח סַח סַח</td></tr>
<tr><td>גֶּפֶן גֶּפֶן</td><td>יָפֶה יָפֶה</td><td>פֶּסַח פֶּסַח</td></tr>
</table>

8 Draw a line from the picture to the correct holiday.

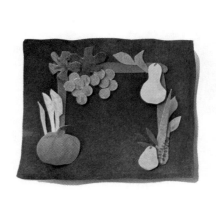
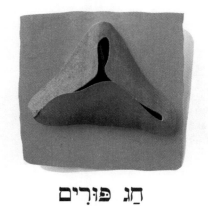
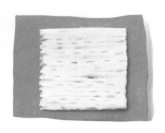

חַג פּוּרִים

חַג הַפֶּסַח

חַג סֻכּוֹת

חַג הַחֲנֻכָּה

יוֹם כִּפּוּר

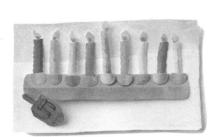
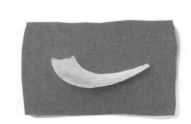

9 Circle the one of two words on the left which goes together with the words in the box.

<table>
<tr><td>יֶלֶד
יְלָדִים</td><td>יַלְדָּה
יוֹם</td><td>יוֹם א
יוֹם ב</td><td>יוֹם ג
סִדּוּר</td></tr>
<tr><td>סֻכּוֹת
בָּאִים</td><td>פּוּרִים
פֶּסַח</td><td>חֲנֻכָּה
חֲנֻכִּיָּה</td><td>הַגָּדָה
נֵר</td></tr>
<tr><td>לֹא
יַלְדָּה</td><td>אַבָּא
אִמָּא</td><td>חֲנֻכָּה
פֶּסַח</td><td>פּוּרִים
אֲנִי</td></tr>
</table>

97

10 Learn these words.

pretty, beautiful, f. (*yafah*) יָפָה   handsome, nice, m. (*yafeh*) יָפֶה

11 Check the correct answer.

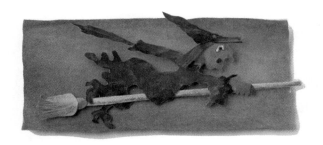

- [ ] יָפָה וְטוֹבָה
- [ ] יָפָה וְלֹא טוֹבָה
- [ ] טוֹבָה וְלֹא יָפָה
- [ ] לֹא טוֹבָה וְלֹא יָפָה

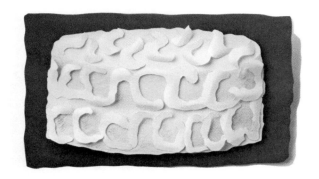

- [ ] יָפָה וְטוֹבָה
- [ ] לֹא יָפָה וְלֹא טוֹבָה
- [ ] יָפָה וְלֹא טוֹבָה
- [ ] טוֹבָה וְלֹא יָפָה

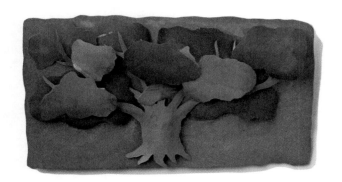

- [ ] יָפֶה וְגָדוֹל
- [ ] יָפֶה וְלֹא גָדוֹל
- [ ] לֹא יָפֶה וְגָדוֹל
- [ ] לֹא יָפֶה וְלֹא גָדוֹל

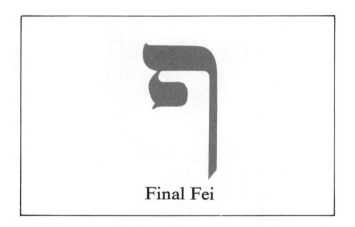

Final Fei

Look at these two letters   פ   ף

The letter ף is written *only* at the *end* of the word.

The letter פ is *never* used at the end of the word.

1 In each group, check the line where all the sounds are the same.

עָיֵף	עוֹף	עָיֵף	☐		חוֹף	חוֹף	חוֹף	☐		אַף	אַף	אַף	☐
סוֹף	סוֹד	סוֹף	☐		עוֹף	נוֹף	עוֹף	☐		גוּף	אַף	גוּף	☐
דַף	דַף	דַף	☐		סוֹף	סוֹף	סוֹף	☐		דַף	תַף	דַף	☐

2 Here are the final letters you already know:

final Chaf   ך,   final Mem   ם,   final Nun   ן,   and final Fei   ף.

3 Read aloud:

גֶפֶן	גֶפֶ	גֶפֶן	גֵּ		יוֹם	יוֹ	יוֹ		מֶלֶךְ	כַּךְ	כַ
אָמֵן	אָמֵ	אָמֵן	אָ		לֶחֶם	לֶחֶ	לְ			מֶלֶ	מֶ
יָחֵף	יָחֵ	יָחֵף	יָ		עוֹף					סוֹף	סוֹ

4 Match.

Fei	פ		Kaf	כ		ם	כ
Pei	פּ		Final Chaf	ך		ן	מ
Final Fei	ף		Chaf	ך		ד	נ
						ף	פ

99

בּוֹרֵא פְּרִי הַגָּפֶן

Borei Peri Hagafen

The Jewish custom is to say a blessing before one enjoys food or drink. This is done especially on יוֹם טוֹב and Shabbat.

You already know the בְּרָכָה for bread which is called הַמּוֹצִיא:

בָּרוּךְ אַתָּה אֲדֹנָי אֱלֹהֵינוּ מֶלֶךְ הָעוֹלָם
הַמּוֹצִיא לֶחֶם מִן הָאָרֶץ

Here is a בְּרָכָה recited upon the drinking of wine:

בָּרוּךְ אַתָּה אֲדֹנָי אֱלֹהֵינוּ מֶלֶךְ הָעוֹלָם
Borei Peri Hagafen   בּוֹרֵא פְּרִי הַגָּפֶן

Creator of the fruit of the vine

Check the sentences which are parts of blessings.

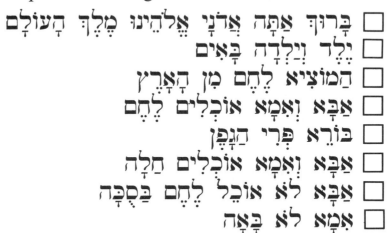

☐ בָּרוּךְ אַתָּה אֲדֹנָי אֱלֹהֵינוּ מֶלֶךְ הָעוֹלָם
☐ יֶלֶד וְיַלְדָּה בָּאִים
☐ הַמּוֹצִיא לֶחֶם מִן הָאָרֶץ
☐ אַבָּא וְאִמָּא אוֹכְלִים לֶחֶם
☐ בּוֹרֵא פְּרִי הַגָּפֶן
☐ אַבָּא וְאִמָּא אוֹכְלִים חַלָּה
☐ אַבָּא לֹא אוֹכֵל לֶחֶם בַּסֻּכָּה
☐ אִמָּא לֹא בָּאָה

A Bingo Card with Hebrew Words

At the end of this book, you will find Hebrew words arranged in squares. Cut out each of the squares and mix them well. Now choose any 24 of the cut-outs and arrange and glue them on a card to play the Bingo game.

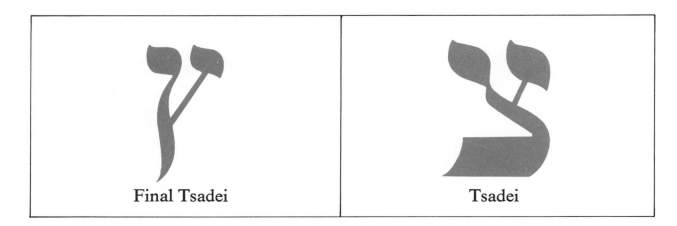

Final Tsadei	Tsadei

1 This is the letter Tsadei צ

The English alphabet does not have a letter for צ.
It sounds a little like tz as in Matzah.

2 Circle the letter Tsadei.

מִצְוָה   בַּת מִצְוָה   בַּר מִצְוָה   מַצָּה   הַמּוֹצִיא

3 The letter צ is written this way:

first this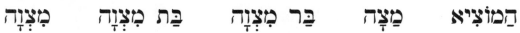
then this
Practice writing the צ.

___   ___   ___   ___   ___   ___

4 Here are the vowels you know. Write them with the letter צ.

Kamats ָ and Patach ַ
Tserei ֵ and Segol ֶ
Cholam with Vav וֹ and without Vav ֹ
Chirik with Yod ִי and without Yod ִ
Shuruk וּ and Kubuts ֻ
Sheva ְ

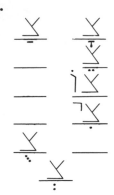

101

5 Check those groups in which all the words are the same.

☐ צִוָּנוּ   צִוָּנוּ   צִוָּנוּ   ☐ מַצָּה   מַצָּה   מַצָּה
☐ מִצְוָה   מִצְווֹת   מִצְוָה   ☐ מַצָּה   מִצּוֹת   מַצָּה
☐ הַמוֹצִיא   הַמוֹצִיא   הַמוֹצִיא   ☐ צֶאנָה   צֶאנָה   צֶאנָה

6 Read aloud:

מַצָּה   מַ   צִוָּנוּ   צִוָ   צַ
מִצּוֹת   מַ   מִצְוָה   מִצְ
הַמוֹצִיא   הַמוֹ   הַ   מִצְווֹת   מִצְ

7 Study these words.

matzot   מַצּוֹת   matzah   מַצָּה

8 Check the correct answers (more than one sentence can be correct).

מִי אוֹכֵל מַצָּה ?

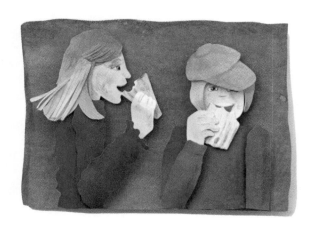

☐ אַבָּא אוֹכֵל לֶחֶם
☐ אִמָא אוֹכֶלֶת לֶחֶם
☐ יֶלֶד אוֹכֵל מַצָּה
☐ יְלָדִים אוֹכְלִים מַצָּה
☐ יַלְדָה אוֹכֶלֶת מַצָּה

9 Circle the words which describe things you can eat.

מַצּוֹת   אַבָּא   אִמָא   נֵר   מַצָּה   נֵרוֹת
יַלְדָה   חַלָה   יֶלֶד   לֶחֶם   מַצָּה   הַגָדָה

10 This is the final Tsadei ץ

The final Tsadei is written this way:

first this

then this

Practice the ץ.

___   ___   ___   ___   ↯   ↯

11 Circle the final letters.

בָּרוּךְ בְּרָכָה מֶלֶךְ בְּרָכוֹת	ךְ
יוֹם מַצָּה יְלָדִים הַמּוֹצִיא אוֹכְלִים	ם
אָמֵן נֵר גֶּפֶן נֵרוֹת מִנְיָן	ן
גוּף גֶּפֶן עוֹף עוּפִי	ף
מַצָּה חָמֵץ אֶרֶץ הַמּוֹצִיא מִצְווֹת	ץ

12 Match.

Final Mem	ך		ם	כ
Final Chaf	ם		ך	מ
Final Nun	ן		ז	נ
Final Tsadei	ף		ץ	פ
Final Fei	ץ		ף	צ

Now you know all of the final letters in Hebrew.

13 Match.

Samech	ע	Kaf	ל	Vav	ז	Alef	בּ
Ayin	ס	Lamed	כּ	Zayin	ו	Bet	א
Pei	פּ	Mem	נ	Chet	ט	Gimel	ד
Tsadei	צ	Nun	מ	Tet	י	Dalet	ה
				Yod	ח	Hei	ג

103

מַצָּה	חָמֵץ
Unleavened Bread	Leavened Bread

On חַג הַפֶּסַח we eat an unleavened bread מַצָּה. The מַצָּה is a reminder of the haste in which the Israelites left Egypt. They had no time to wait for their bread לֶחֶם to rise.

On the eve of פֶּסַח, an old custom is to get rid of all bread and other foods that might have leavening חָמֵץ. Many Jews light a candle נֵר and search for food which is חָמֵץ. If they find a piece of bread, they sweep it up with a feather into a wooden spoon to be burned the next morning.

On the Seder night, the youngest child asks the Four Questions about חַג הַפֶּסַח. The Four Questions begin with the words *Mah Nishtanah*.

Here is the first question of the *Mah Nishtanah* מַה נִשְׁתַּנָה:

Mah nishtanah	מַה נִשְׁתַּנָה
Halayelah hazeh	הַלַּיְלָה הַזֶּה
Mikol haleilot?	מִכָּל הַלֵּילוֹת ?
Shebechol haleilot	שֶׁבְּכָל הַלֵּילוֹת
Anu ochelin	אָנוּ אוֹכְלִין
Chamets umatzah.	חָמֵץ וּמַצָּה.
Halayelah hazeh	הַלַּיְלָה הַזֶּה
Kulo matzah	כֻּלּוֹ מַצָּה

Why is this
Night different
From all other nights?
On all other nights
We eat
Leavened bread and matzah.
On this night
only matzah

104

1 The *Mah Nishtanah* has several melodies. Do you know one of them?

2 Find the *Mah Nishtanah* in the הַגָּדָה. Your teacher will help you read it.

3 Fill in the correct words.

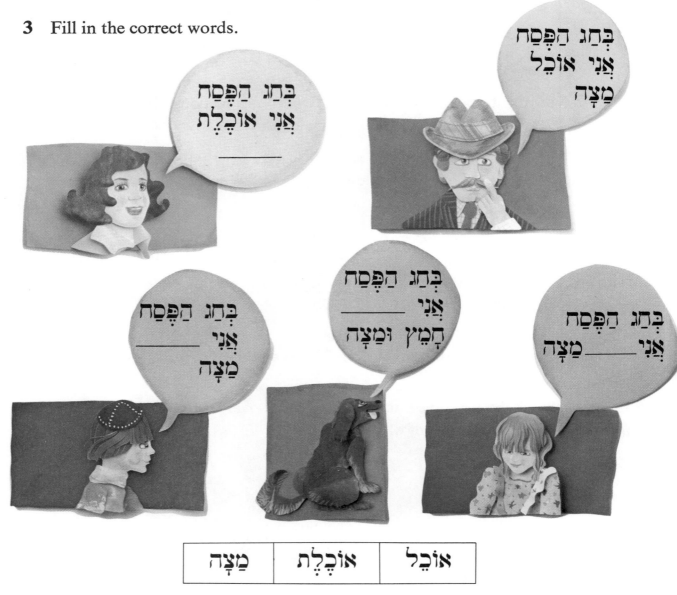

מַצָּה	אוֹכֶלֶת	אוֹכֵל

4 Read aloud:

אַבָּא טוֹב וְיָפֶה
יֶלֶד טוֹב וְיָפֶה
חֶדֶר טוֹב וְיָפֶה
לֶחֶם טוֹב
לֶחֶם יָפֶה

אִמָּא טוֹבָה וְיָפָה
יַלְדָּה טוֹבָה וְיָפָה
סֻכָּה טוֹבָה וְיָפָה
חַלָּה טוֹבָה
מַצָּה יָפָה

מִצְווֹת Mitzvot	מִצְוָה Mitzvah
בַּת מִצְוָה Bat Mitzvah	בַּר מִצְוָה Bar Mitzvah

On his thirteenth birthday a Jewish boy becomes responsible for his deeds. He is בַּר מִצְוָה son of the commandment.

On her thirteenth birthday, a Jewish girl is בַּת מִצְוָה, responsible for her own actions and behavior.

On the Bar or Bat Mitzvah day, the boy or the girl, honored in the synagogue with an עֲלִיָה, goes up to the pulpit, says the blessings over the Torah, and reads the Haftarah.

This says: We accept the spirit of the Torah and the מִצְווֹת.

Lighting the Shabbat candles, saying the בְּרָכָה over the נֵרוֹת on Shabbat eve, is one of the most important of the מִצְווֹת.

Baruch Atah	בָּרוּךְ אַתָּה
Adonai Elohenu	אֲדֹנָי אֱלֹהֵינוּ
Melech ha'olam	מֶלֶךְ הָעוֹלָם
Asher kideshanu bemitzvotav	אֲשֶׁר קִדְּשָׁנוּ בְּמִצְוֹתָיו
Vetsivanu lehadlik	וְצִוָּנוּ לְהַדְלִיק
Ner shel Shabbat	נֵר שֶׁל שַׁבָּת

Blessed is
The Lord our God
Ruler of the universe
Who made us holy with His mitzvot
And commands us to kindle
The lights of Shabbat

106

1 Fill in the missing words in each blessing.

א) בָּרוּךְ אַתָּה אֲדֹנָי אֱלֹהֵינוּ מֶלֶךְ הָעוֹלָם
הַמּוֹצִיא _____ מִן הָאָרֶץ

ב) _____ אַתָּה אֲדֹנָי אֱלֹהֵינוּ מֶלֶךְ הָעוֹלָם
בּוֹרֵא פְּרִי הַגָּפֶן

ג) בָּרוּךְ אַתָּה אֲדֹנָי אֱלֹהֵינוּ _____ הָעוֹלָם

ד) בָּרוּךְ אַתָּה אֲדֹנָי אֱלֹהֵינוּ מֶלֶךְ הָעוֹלָם
אֲשֶׁר קִדְּשָׁנוּ בְּמִצְוֹתָיו וְצִוָּנוּ לְהַדְלִיק
_____ שֶׁל שַׁבָּת

לֶחֶם	בָּרוּךְ	מֶלֶךְ	נֵר

2 Hebrew letters can be used as numbers.

ע = 70	כ = 20	ו = 6	א = 1
פ = __	ל = __	__ = 7	ב = 2
צ = 90	מ = 40	ח = 8	ג = 3
	נ = 50	ט = __	ד = __
	ס = 60	י = 10	ה = 5

3 Which lines have the words in correct alphabetical order?

☐ אָמֵן   בְּרָכָה   חַלָּה   לֶחֶם   מִצְוָה

☐ אָמֵן   בְּרָכָה   לֶחֶם   חַלָּה   מִצְוָה

☐ סִדוּר   פֶּסַח   עֲלִיָּה   נֵר   צַדִּיקִים

☐ נֵר   סִדוּר   עֲלִיָּה   פֶּסַח   צַדִּיקִים

ל"ו צַדִּיקִים
Lamed-Vav Tsadikim

A legend says there are thirty-six righteous people צַדִּיקִים in the world. When one dies, another *tsadik* replaces that one.

The legend says that without the thirty-six *tsadikim* the world would come to an end since the world exists because of the thirty-six.

In Hebrew, we call them ל"ו צַדִּיקִים (Lamed-Vav = 36).

There are many stories about the ל"ו צַדִּיקִים — stories about their joy in helping others and their joy in praying to God.

Most of the ל"ו צַדִּיקִים are not rabbis. Many are not even learned Jews. Some don't know the Torah well and are unable to read the prayers. They are humble and simple people.

No one knows who these ל"ו צַדִּיקִים are. Even they themselves don't know how important they are.

There is a story about a great rabbi who came to the synagogue on the eve of Yom Kippur יוֹם כִּפּוּר. It was time to begin the service and chant the Kol Nidrei, but the rabbi did not begin.

He stood at the pulpit, his eyes shut as if he were listening to a secret voice. The congregation stood silently waiting for the rabbi to begin. A long time passed. And finally the rabbi began chanting the Kol Nidrei.

When the service was over, the people asked the rabbi: "What happened? What made you wait so long?"

108

"One of the לֹ"ו צַדִיקִים was in the synagogue with us tonight," said the rabbi. "He could not read the prayers in Hebrew. He could only say the Alef-Bet. So that is the way he prayed. He said it again and again with all his heart. The letters reached up to God, and there all His servants were busy putting the letters together and making beautiful new prayers out of them."

The rabbi delayed the Yom Kippur service so that it would not interfere with the Alef-Bet prayer of one of the לֹ"ו צַדִיקִים.

1 Do you know another story about a צַדִיק?

2 Hebrew letters are sometimes used for numbers:
36 righteous people   לֹ"ו צַדִיקִים

3 Find out what is meant by Tu Bishvat and Lag Ba'omer.

ט"ו בִּשְׁבָט _____

_____

_____

לַ"ג בָּעֹמֶר _____

_____

_____

4 You may hear people say: "I am going to give חַי dollars to Hadassah."
How much is חַי? _____

109

Review Test

1 Circle the correct word.   (1 point each)

nice, girl, bad	יָפֶה	mother, father, child	אַבָּא
big, beautiful, bad	יָפָה	mother, father, girl	אִמָּא
bread, chalah, matzah	לֶחֶם	boy, mother, girl	יַלְדָה
yes, no, good	לֹא	bread, blessing, matzah	בְּרָכָה
bread, chalah, matzah	מַצָה	small, nice, big	גָדוֹל
matzah, matzot, mitzvah	מַצוֹת	prayer welcoming	הַבְדָלָה
matzah, matzot, mitzvah	מִצְוָה	Shabbat, prayer saying	
good, m.; good, f.	טוֹבָה	goodbye to Shabbat	
book, prayer book,	סִדוּר	food, luck, holiday	חַג
Haggadah		candle, candles, light	נֵר
what, where, who	מִי	blessing over bread,	הַמוֹצִיא
		blessing over wine	
		Purim, Chanukah, Sukot	חֲנֻכָּה

(Total: 20 points)

2 Check the sentences which are part of prayers.   (3 points each)

☐ הַמוֹצִיא לֶחֶם מִן הָאָרֶץ

☐ יֶלֶד וְיַלְדָה אוֹכְלִים חַלָה

☐ בּוֹרֵא פְּרִי הַגֶפֶן

☐ מִי הַיַלְדָה הַיָפָה ?

☐ לְהַדְלִיק נֵר שֶׁל חֲנֻכָּה

☐ דָג גָדוֹל וְטוֹב

☐ בָּרוּךְ אַתָּה אֲדֹנָי

☐ הַיְלָדִים בָּאִים

☐ לְהַדְלִיק נֵר שֶׁל שַׁבָּת

☐ הַיַלְדָה אוֹכֶלֶת מַצָה

(Total: 30 points)

110

3 Check the correct answer. (8 points each)

☐ הַיֶּלֶד הַגָּדוֹל אוֹכֵל חַלָּה
☐ הַיַּלְדָּה אוֹכֶלֶת חַלָּה
☐ אִמָּא אוֹכֶלֶת מַצָּה
☐ אַבָּא וְהַיֶּלֶד אוֹכְלִים מַצָּה

☐ חַג הַחֲנֻכָּה
☐ חַג פּוּרִים
☐ חַג הַפֶּסַח
☐ יוֹם כִּפּוּר

(Total: 16 points)

Crossword Puzzle

Down
5. mother
6. children
7. Hamotzi
8. day

Across
1. father
2. eat
3. girl
4. I

(4 points for each correct word)

אַבָּא	יַלְדָּה	אֲנִי
הַמּוֹצִיא	אוֹכְלִים	אִמָּא
	יְלָדִים	יוֹם

(Total: 32 points)

(2 bonus points for a perfect score)

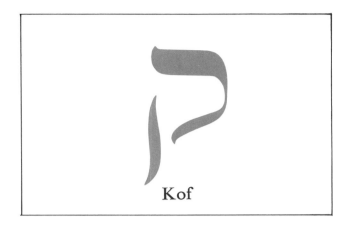

Kof

1 This is the letter Kof ק

It has the sound of K as in Kiddush and Tsadikim.

2 Circle the letter Kof: קָדוֹשׁ צַדִּיק צַדִּיקִים מְקַדֵּשׁ הַשַּׁבָּת

3 The letter ק is written this way:

first this   then this

Practice writing the ק.

— — — — — ֵ ד

4 Read aloud:

קֹ	קֹ	קֹי	קֹי		קֵ	קֵ	קַ
קָה	קָה	קָא	קָא		קֵ	קֵ	קִ
קָ	קִ	קֵ	קֵ		קֹ	קוֹ	קֹ

5 In each group, circle the word which sounds different from the others.

קַל	קוֹל	קוֹל	הַדְלִיקוּ	לְהַדְלִיק	לְהַדְלִיק
לְהַדְלִיק	צַדִּיק	לְהַדְלִיק	צַדִּיק	צַדִּיקִים	צַדִּיק
צַדִּיקִים	לְהַדְלִיק	צַדִּיקִים	צְדָקָה	צְדָקָה	צֶדֶק
קַל	קוֹלִי	קוֹלִי	צַדִּיקִים	צַדִּיק	צַדִּיקִים

112

There is an old story called "A Dog and a Prince," which tells about Jewish life in a ghetto in Russia. The story is about a poor man whose job was to carry water from the river. During the weekdays, he lived "like a dog," but, on the eve of Shabbat, the so-called dog turned into a prince....

The Shabbat made him feel special and holy and helped him forget his hard life.

On Erev Shabbat the קִדּוּשׁ is chanted. קִדּוּשׁ means "making holy."

The *Kiddush* begins with the words:

Vayehi erev	וַיְהִי עֶרֶב
Vayehi voker	וַיְהִי בֹקֶר
Yom hashishi.	יוֹם הַשִּׁשִּׁי.
Vayechulu	וַיְכֻלּוּ
Hashamayim veha'aretz	הַשָּׁמַיִם וְהָאָרֶץ
Vechol tseva'am	וְכָל צְבָאָם

And it was evening
And it was morning of
The sixth day.
And they were finished making
The heaven and the earth
And all their host

The *Kiddush* speaks about the reason for celebrating the Shabbat:

And God blessed the seventh day and made it holy,
Because He rested on it from all His work.

113

The קִדּוּשׁ ends with a sentence about making the Shabbat holy:

Baruch Atah Adonai	בָּרוּךְ אַתָּה אֲדֹנָי
Mekadesh Hashabbat	מְקַדֵּשׁ הַשַׁבָּת

Blessed is the Lord
For the Sabbath and its holiness

The קִדּוּשׁ ceremony is a way of saying that the ordinary days are ending and the holy Shabbat is beginning.

The Shabbat ends with a special ceremony called הַבְדָלָה.

The הַבְדָלָה, or separation ceremony, is a way of saying that the holy day has come to an end and the ordinary days of the week are again beginning.

1 Check the sentences which are part of a blessing or prayer.

☐ בָּרוּךְ אַתָּה אֲדֹנָי מְקַדֵּשׁ הַשַׁבָּת

☐ אַבָּא אוֹכֵל לֶחֶם

☐ הַמַבְדִיל בֵּין קֹדֶשׁ לְחוֹל

☐ אַבָּא בָּא וְאִמָּא בָּאָה

☐ הַמוֹצִיא לֶחֶם מִן הָאָרֶץ

☐ אִמָּא אוֹכֶלֶת חַלָה טוֹבָה

☐ בּוֹרֵא פְּרִי הַגֶּפֶן

☐ וְצִוָּנוּ לְהַדְלִיק נֵר שֶׁל שַׁבָּת

☐ וְצִוָּנוּ לְהַדְלִיק נֵר שֶׁל חֲנֻכָּה

☐ אַבָּא וְהַיְלָדִים אוֹכְלִים מַצָּה טוֹבָה

2 Invite the cantor, the rabbi, or a member of your congregation to chant the קִדּוּשׁ and הַבְדָלָה.

What do you have to prepare for their visit?

_____

_____

בְּרָכוֹת

Berachot—Blessings

1   Fill in the missing words in these prayers.

א)   בָּרוּךְ אַתָּה אֲדֹנָי אֱלֹהֵינוּ מֶלֶךְ הָעוֹלָם
הַמּוֹצִיא _____ מִן הָאָרֶץ (לֶחֶם חַלָּה)

ב)   בָּרוּךְ אַתָּה אֲדֹנָי אֱלֹהֵינוּ מֶלֶךְ הָעוֹלָם
בּוֹרֵא פְּרִי _____ (מֶלֶךְ הַגָּפֶן)

ג)   _____ אַתָּה אֲדֹנָי מְקַדֵּשׁ הַשַּׁבָּת (בָּרוּךְ בְּרָכוֹת)

2   Read these blessings בְּרָכוֹת aloud:

Blessed is the Lord our God	בָּרוּךְ אַתָּה אֲדֹנָי אֱלֹהֵינוּ
Ruler of the universe	מֶלֶךְ הָעוֹלָם
Who causes bread to come	הַמּוֹצִיא לֶחֶם
From the earth	מִן הָאָרֶץ
Blessed is the Lord our God	בָּרוּךְ אַתָּה אֲדֹנָי אֱלֹהֵינוּ
Ruler of the universe	מֶלֶךְ הָעוֹלָם
Creator of the fruit of the vine	בּוֹרֵא פְּרִי הַגָּפֶן

3   Now you see how a בְּרָכָה begins.

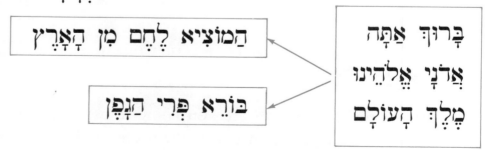

4 You can use the same beginning and say other בְּרָכוֹת.

A blessing בְּרָכָה when you eat fruits from trees

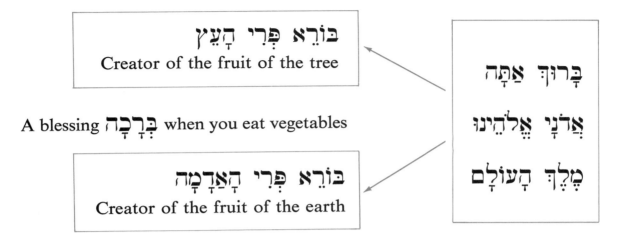

בּוֹרֵא פְּרִי הָעֵץ
Creator of the fruit of the tree

A blessing בְּרָכָה when you eat vegetables

בּוֹרֵא פְּרִי הָאֲדָמָה
Creator of the fruit of the earth

בָּרוּךְ אַתָּה
אֲדֹנָי אֱלֹהֵינוּ
מֶלֶךְ הָעוֹלָם

5 Some בְּרָכוֹת have a longer beginning:

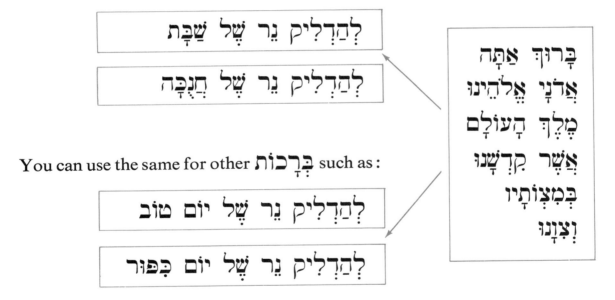

לְהַדְלִיק נֵר שֶׁל שַׁבָּת

לְהַדְלִיק נֵר שֶׁל חֲנֻכָּה

You can use the same for other בְּרָכוֹת such as:

לְהַדְלִיק נֵר שֶׁל יוֹם טוֹב

לְהַדְלִיק נֵר שֶׁל יוֹם כִּפּוּר

בָּרוּךְ אַתָּה
אֲדֹנָי אֱלֹהֵינוּ
מֶלֶךְ הָעוֹלָם
אֲשֶׁר קִדְּשָׁנוּ
בְּמִצְוֹתָיו
וְצִוָּנוּ

6 Join a committee and make a poster of one of the בְּרָכוֹת or part of a בְּרָכָה.

What kind of materials are you going to use? Do you have some original ideas? Do you want to decorate the poster with a picture?

116

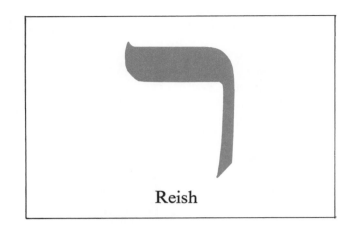

Reish

1 This is the letter Reish ר

It has the sound of R as in Rosh Hashanah, Yom Kippur, and Purim.

2 The letter ר, like many other Hebrew letters, is a picture of a word. It resembles the word Rosh which means "head."

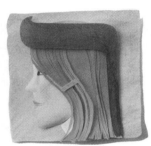

3 Circle the letter Reish.

רֹאשׁ הַשָּׁנָה   יוֹם כִּפּוּר   פּוּרִים   בּוֹרֵא פְּרִי הַגָּפֶן

בְּרָכָה   בְּרָכוֹת   בָּרוּךְ   נֵר   נֵרוֹת

4 Practice writing the ר.

___ ___ ___ ___ ר ר

5 Read aloud:

יוֹם כִּפּוּר   פּוּרִים   נֵר   נֵרוֹת   פְּרִי

בַּר מִצְוָה   סִדוּר   בְּרָכָה   בְּרָכוֹת   בָּרוּךְ

בּוֹרֵא פְּרִי הַגָּפֶן

לְהַדְלִיק נֵר שֶׁל חֲנֻכָּה

בָּרוּךְ אַתָּה אֲדֹנָי

117

6 Circle the one of two words on the left which goes together with the words
in the box.

יֶלֶד יוֹם כִּפּוּר	יַלְדָּה יְלָדִים	חַג הַפֶּסַח יַלְדָּה	יוֹם כִּפּוּר חֲנֻכָּה
סִדּוּר אוֹכְלִים	אוֹכֵל אוֹכֶלֶת	אַבָּא חֲנֻכָּה	נֵר נֵרוֹת
יוֹם ג קָדוֹשׁ	יוֹם א יוֹם ב	נֵרוֹת בָּאִים	בָּא בָּאָה
חַלָּה רֹאשׁ הַשָּׁנָה	מַצָּה לֶחֶם	סִדּוּר יַלְדָּה	אַבָּא אִמָּא

7 Check those sentences which describe the picture.

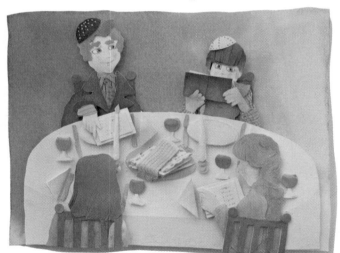

☐ מַצּוֹת   ☐ חַג הַפֶּסַח

☐ אַבָּא אִמָּא וִילָדִים   ☐ חַג פּוּרִים

☐ יַלְדָּה אוֹכֶלֶת בַּסֻּכָּה   ☐ יוֹם כִּפּוּר

☐ הַגָּדָה   ☐ אַבָּא אוֹכֵל לֶחֶם

☐ אַבָּא אִמָּא יֶלֶד וְיַלְדָּה   ☐ יַלְדָּה אוֹכֶלֶת לֶחֶם

☐ נֵר וַחֲנֻכִּיָה   ☐ חַג הַסֻּכּוֹת

118

8 Can you tell the difference between the letter ר and the letter ד?

Trace the letter ר with a colored pen or pencil.

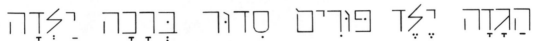

Now trace the letter ד with another color.

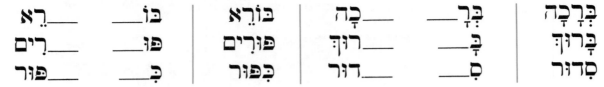

9 Fill in the missing part of the word.

בּוֹ___	___רֵא	בּוֹרֵא	___כָה	בְּרָ___	בְּרָכָה
___פֿוּ	___רִים	פּוּרִים	___רוּךְ	בָּ___	בָּרוּךְ
כְּ___	___פּוֹר	כְּפֿוֹר	___דוּר	___ס	סִדוּר

Crossword Puzzle

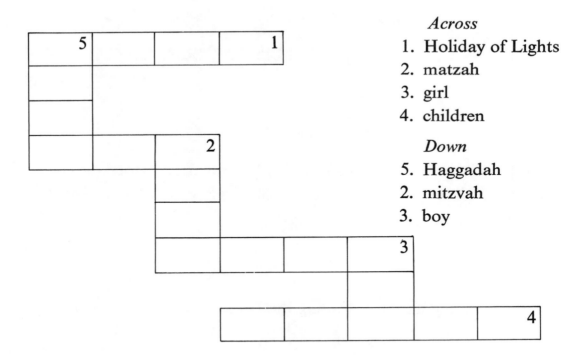

Across

1. Holiday of Lights
2. matzah
3. girl
4. children

Down

5. Haggadah
2. mitzvah
3. boy

מַצָּה	חֲנֻכָּה	יְלָדִים	יֶלֶד	יַלְדָּה	מִצְוָה	הַגָּדָה

119

Birkat Hamazon—Grace after the Meal

The blessings בְּרָכוֹת make every meal a special event. By saying a בְּרָכָה we are not simply eating food—we are having a celebration.

When bread לֶחֶם is to be eaten at a meal, the custom is to recite *Hamotzi*:

בָּרוּךְ אַתָּה אֲדֹנָי אֱלֹהֵינוּ מֶלֶךְ הָעוֹלָם
הַמּוֹצִיא לֶחֶם מִן הָאָרֶץ

When we drink wine or grape juice, we say the blessing בְּרָכָה:

בָּרוּךְ אַתָּה אֲדֹנָי אֱלֹהֵינוּ מֶלֶךְ הָעוֹלָם
בּוֹרֵא פְּרִי הַגָּפֶן

The custom, however, is to say a בְּרָכָה not only before the meal. There is also a בְּרָכָה at the end of the meal. It is called the *Birkat Hamazon*. בִּרְכַּת הַמָּזוֹן is the Grace after the Meal.

We often give the honor of leading the בִּרְכַּת הַמָּזוֹן to a guest.

Ask your teacher, your rabbi, or your cantor to chant the *Birkat Hamazon* בִּרְכַּת הַמָּזוֹן.

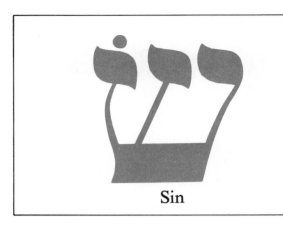

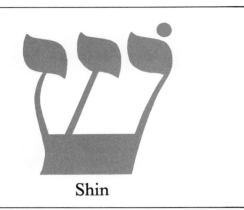

Sin — Shin

1 This is the letter Shin שׁ

It has the sound Sh as in Shema, Shabbat, and Kiddush.

2 Circle the letter Shin.

שְׁמַע יִשְׂרָאֵל   שַׁבָּת שָׁלוֹם   מְקַדֵּשׁ הַשַׁבָּת
רֹאשׁ הַשָׁנָה   נֵר שֶׁל שַׁבָּת   קָדוֹשׁ

3 Read aloud:

שַׁבָּת שָׁלוֹם   שַׁבָּת שָׁלוֹם
רֹאשׁ הַשָׁנָה   שָׁנָה טוֹבָה

שָׁנָה טוֹבָה, אַבָּא
שָׁנָה טוֹבָה, אִמָא

4 The letter Shin שׁ has a sister Sin שׂ

What is the difference between the two letters?

_____

_____

The letter שׂ has the sound of S as in Israel and Small.

121

5 Trace the letter Shin with one color and the letter Sin with another.

שְׁמַע יִשְׂרָאֵל אֶרֶץ שָׁלוֹם שַׁבָּת יִשְׂרָאֵל

רֹאשׁ הַשָּׁנָה שָׁנָה טוֹבָה חַג שָׂמֵחַ

6 The letter שׁ is written this way:

first this

then this

Practice writing the שׁ.

_____ _____ _____ _____ ‫�‫ �

Practice writing the שׂ.

_____ _____ _____ _____ ‫ �

Practice writing both שׁ and שׂ.

_____ _____ _____ _____ ‫ �

7 Fill in the missing part of the word.

_____אֵל	_____יִשְׂרָ	יִשְׂרָאֵל
_____לוֹם	שָׁ_____	שָׁלוֹם
_____נָה	שָׁ_____	שָׁנָה

8 Here are the sister letters:

שׂ שׁ   פ פּ   כ כּ   ב בּ

The sister letters do not sound alike.
The letters פּ, כּ, and בּ have a _____ inside the letter.
The letter שׁ has a dot on the right.
The letter שׂ has a dot on the _____.

122

9 Match.

Vet	כ	Bet	פ
Chaf	ב	Kaf	בּ
Fei	שׁ	Pei	כּ
Sin	פּ	Shin	שׂ

כ	בּ
בּ	כּ
שׁ	שׂ
פּ	שׁ

מַזָּל טוֹב. You now know all the sister letters.

10 Check the line where all the sounds are alike.

☐ שָׁבוּ שָׁבוּ שָׁבוּ   ☐ שׁוּ שׁוּ שׁוּ
☐ עָשֶׂר עָשֶׂר עָשֶׂר   ☐ שׁוּ שׁוּ שִׂי
☐ עָשָׂה עָשָׂה עָשׂוּ   ☐ שָׁשׁ שָׁשׁ שִׂשִׂי
☐ שְׁמַע שְׁמַע שְׁמַע   ☐ שַׁבָּת שַׁבָּת שָׁנָה

11 Circle the words which describe things that you can eat.

בְּרָכָה   שַׁבָּת   חַלָּה   שָׁלוֹם
נֵר   נֵרוֹת   חֲנֻכִּיָּה   לֶחֶם
רֹאשׁ הַשָּׁנָה   פּוּרִים   פֶּסַח   מַצָּה
חַג הַסֻּכּוֹת   סֻכָּה   מַצּוֹת   חֲנֻכָּה

12 Circle the words which stand for people.

שַׁבָּת שָׁלוֹם   בְּרָכוֹת   שַׁבָּת
רֹאשׁ הַשָּׁנָה   חַג הַפֶּסַח   יַלְדָּה
יֶלֶד   בְּרָכָה   יְלָדִים   חַג הַסֻּכּוֹת
מִצְוָה   מִצְווֹת   אַבָּא   מַצָּה
מַצּוֹת   אִמָּא   סֻכָּה   לֶחֶם

123

רֹאשׁ הַשָּׁנָה

Rosh Hashanah

1   Read aloud:

רֹאשׁ הַשָּׁנָה בָּא | שָׁנָה טוֹבָה, יְלָדִים
שָׁנָה טוֹבָה, אַבָּא | שָׁנָה טוֹבָה !
שָׁנָה טוֹבָה, אִמָּא

2   Make your own שָׁנָה טוֹבָה card.

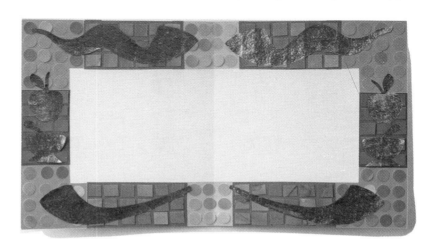

שְׁמַע יִשְׂרָאֵל

Shema Yisrael

Shema Yisrael שְׁמַע יִשְׂרָאֵל are two very old and very important Hebrew words. They are written in the Torah and are recited by Jews all over the world every day of the year.

Jews say שְׁמַע יִשְׂרָאֵל during the most important moments of their lives— when they pray; when they celebrate holy days; during happy events; and when they need help.

Saying שְׁמַע יִשְׂרָאֵל gives Jews the feeling of being one with all other Jews throughout the world.

Find the prayer שְׁמַע יִשְׂרָאֵל in the סִדּוּר. Ask your teacher to read it.

שָׁלוֹם

Shalom

One of the best known of all Hebrew words is שָׁלוֹם which has three meanings:
Peace, Hello, Goodbye.

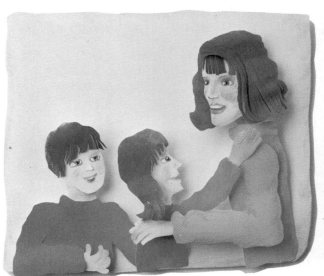

שָׁלוֹם יְלָדִים
שָׁלוֹם אִמָּא

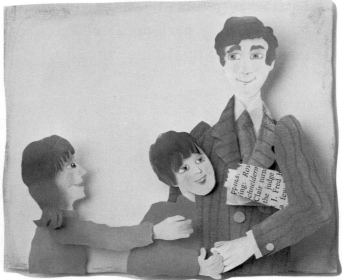

שָׁלוֹם יְלָדִים
שָׁלוֹם אַבָּא

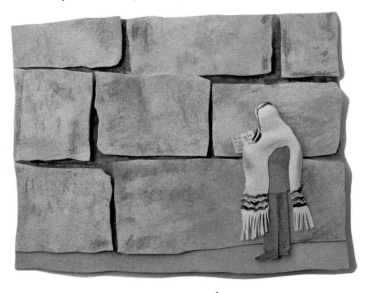

שִׂים שָׁלוֹם טוֹבָה וּבְרָכָה

125

Israeli children have suffered a great deal during their lives. Many have lived through more than one war.

Like all children in the world, they wish for peace more than anything else. But, for them, *Peace* has a very special meaning.

Here is a poem written by an Israeli child after the Yom Kippur War in 1973. It is part of a collection of poems in the book *My Shalom, My Peace* (Tel Aviv, Israel: Sabra Books).

A Prayer for שָׁלוֹם

> What shall I ask You for, God?
> I have everything.
>
>   . . .
>
> I ask only for one thing. . .
> I'd like to ask for Peace.
> Yes, it's Peace I want.
>
>   . . .
>
> You created the Land of Peace,
> Where stands the City of Peace,
> Where stood the Temple of Peace,
> But where still there is no Peace. . . .
>
> Peace is what I ask for,
> Only Peace.
>   Shlomit Grossberg
>   Age 13, Jerusalem

Even when Jewish people in Israel are forced to fight and defend themselves, they continue to hope for peace.

126

Here is one of the most popular peace songs:

Hevenu Shalom Aleichem הֲבֵאנוּ שָׁלוֹם עֲלֵיכֶם

Peace Be to You

הֲבֵאנוּ שָׁלוֹם עֲלֵיכֶם !

הֲבֵאנוּ שָׁלוֹם עֲלֵיכֶם !

הֲבֵאנוּ שָׁלוֹם עֲלֵיכֶם !

הֲבֵאנוּ שָׁלוֹם, שָׁלוֹם,

שָׁלוֹם עֲלֵיכֶם !

Shabbat is sometimes described as a queen who arrives on erev Shabbat surrounded by angels of peace מַלְאֲכֵי הַשָּׁלוֹם.

As the members of the family sit around the table lighted with Shabbat candles נֵרוֹת שַׁבָּת, they imagine that the angels of peace enter the house.

The family sings:

Enter in peace, O messengers of peace מַלְאֲכֵי הַשָּׁלוֹם
Bless me with peace, O messengers of peace מַלְאֲכֵי הַשָּׁלוֹם

And as the angels leave the house, the family sings:

Depart in peace, O messenger of peace מַלְאֲכֵי הַשָּׁלוֹם

127

Here is the complete song. You can find it in your prayer book סִדּוּר.

שָׁלוֹם עֲלֵיכֶם

Peace be to you,   שָׁלוֹם עֲלֵיכֶם,

O helping messengers   מַלְאֲכֵי הַשָּׁרֵת

Messengers of the Most High   מַלְאֲכֵי עֶלְיוֹן

The supreme King of kings   מִמֶּלֶךְ מַלְכֵי הַמְּלָכִים

The Holy One, blessed be He   הַקָּדוֹשׁ, בָּרוּךְ הוּא

Enter in Peace,   בּוֹאֲכֶם לְשָׁלוֹם,

O messengers of peace   מַלְאֲכֵי הַשָּׁלוֹם

Messengers of the Most High   מַלְאֲכֵי עֶלְיוֹן

The supreme King of kings   מִמֶּלֶךְ מַלְכֵי הַמְּלָכִים

The Holy One, blessed be He   הַקָּדוֹשׁ, בָּרוּךְ הוּא

Bless me in peace,   בָּרְכוּנִי לְשָׁלוֹם,

O messengers of peace   מַלְאֲכֵי הַשָּׁלוֹם

Messengers of the Most High   מַלְאֲכֵי עֶלְיוֹן

The supreme King of kings   מִמֶּלֶךְ מַלְכֵי הַמְּלָכִים

The Holy One, blessed be He   הַקָּדוֹשׁ, בָּרוּךְ הוּא

Depart in peace,   צֵאתְכֶם לְשָׁלוֹם,

O messengers of peace   מַלְאֲכֵי הַשָּׁלוֹם

Messengers of the Most High   מַלְאֲכֵי עֶלְיוֹן

The supreme King of kings   מִמֶּלֶךְ מַלְכֵי הַמְּלָכִים

The Holy One, blessed be He   הַקָּדוֹשׁ, בָּרוּךְ הוּא

This is a song of peace. One important idea that we remember on Shabbat is the desire to have peace.

When the Shabbat prayers are over, we turn to our neighbors in the synagogue and say שַׁבָּת שָׁלוֹם.

Having שָׁלוֹם is more than not having war.

Having שָׁלוֹם is being happy with yourself; being happy with your family and friends.

שָׁלוֹם is to feel peaceful. This is the real message of

שַׁבָּת שָׁלוֹם !

Write a story or a poem or draw a picture describing your feelings about

שָׁלוֹם

How many letters are there in the English alphabet? _____

It is generally said that Hebrew has 22 letters. This is only partly correct. In addition to the 22 letters, Hebrew has:

the final letters and the sister letters

You have learned all the final letters. They are:

ץ ף ן ם ךְ

1 Circle the final letters.

ךְ	בָּרוּךְ בְּרָכָה בְּרָכוֹת מֶלֶךְ
ם	שָׁלוֹם עֲלֵיכֶם יְלָדִים הַמוֹצִיא לֶחֶם מַצָה
ן	אָמֵן בּוֹרֵא פְּרִי הַגָּפֶן נֵרוֹת מִנְיָן
ף	גוּף עוֹף אֲפִיקוֹמָן גֶּפֶן
ץ	מִצְוָה מַצָה חָמֵץ אֶרֶץ יִשְׂרָאֵל עֵץ

2 Match.

Final Chaf	ם	ם	כ
Final Mem	ךְ	ךְ	מ
Final Nun	ף	ף	נ
Final Fei	ן	ץ	פ
Final Tsadei	ץ	ן	צ

130

3 Check the lines where all words are the same.

גֶּפֶן	נֵר	נֵרוֹת ☐		בָּרוּךְ	בָּרוּךְ	בָּרוּךְ ☐
גֶּפֶן	עוֹף	עוֹף ☐		מְלָכִים	מֶלֶךְ	מֶלֶךְ ☐
אֶרֶץ	חָמֵץ	חָמֵץ ☐		שָׁלוֹם	שָׁלוֹם	שָׁלוֹם ☐
אֶרֶץ	אֶרֶץ	אֶרֶץ ☐		עֲלֵיכֶם	עֲלֵיכֶם	עֲלֵיכֶם ☐
				אָמֵן	מִנְיָן	אָמֵן ☐

In addition to the final letters, Hebrew has sister letters:

שׁ שׂ פ פּ כ כּ ב בּ

Remember them by the saying: The Point Makes a Difference.

When you take out the point from the בּ you have _____

When you take out the point from the כּ you have _____

When you take out the point from the פּ you have _____

When you move the point of the שׁ to the left, you have _____

4 Match.

Vet	כ	Bet	כּ	כ	בּ
Chaf	ב	Kaf	בּ	ב	כּ
Fei	שׁ	Pei	שׂ	שׁ	פּ
Sin	פ	Shin	פּ	פ	שׂ

5 In each group, circle the word which is different from the others.

בְּרָכָה	בְּרָכָה	בְּרָכוֹת	בְּרָכָה	בְּרָכוֹת	בְּרָכָה
פֶּסַח	פּוּרִים	פּוּרִים	טוֹב	טוֹבָה	טוֹב
אָמֵן	גֶּפֶן	גֶּפֶן	סֻכּוֹת	סֻכּוֹת	סֻכָּה
קֹדֶשׁ	קָדוֹשׁ	קָדוֹשׁ	שְׁמַע	שָׁלוֹם	שָׁלוֹם
בָּרוּךְ	בְּרָכָה	בָּרוּךְ	יִשְׂרָאֵל	שְׁמַע	יִשְׂרָאֵל
טוֹב	טוֹב	טוֹבָה	יָפֶה	יָפֶה	יָפֶה

131

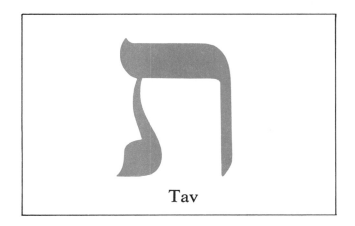

Tav

1 This is the letter Tav ת

It is the last letter of the אָלֶף־בֵּית.
It has the sound of T as in Torah, Matzot, and Tel Aviv.

2 Circle the letter Tav.

מַצּוֹת   תְּפִלָּה   שַׁבָּת   בַּת מִצְוָה   נֵרוֹת   תּוֹרָה

3 The letter Tav is the last letter of the Alef-Bet.
When we say from א to ת, we mean from the beginning to the end.

4 The letter ת is written this way:

first this ⇀↓

then this ↵⌐

Practice writing the letter ת.

____   ____   ____   ____   ⬚   ⊓

5 Here are the vowels you know. Write them with the letter ת.

Kamats ָ and Patach ַ
Tserei ֵ and Segol ֶ
Cholam with Vav וֹ and without Vav ֹ
Chirik with Yod ִי and without Yod ִ
Shuruk וּ and Kubuts ֻ
Sheva ְ

132

6 Read aloud:

בַּת מִצְוָה   מַצּוֹת   מִצְווֹת | תּוֹרָה   שַׁבָּת   נֵרוֹת

סֻכּוֹת   בְּרָכוֹת   אוֹכֶלֶת | בִּרְכַּת הַמָּזוֹן   תּוֹרָה

7 Circle the words which are names of holidays.

רֹאשׁ הַשָּׁנָה   שָׁנָה טוֹבָה   יֶלֶד   פּוּרִים   אִמָּא

מְזוּזָה   יוֹם כִּפּוּר   נֵר   חֲנֻכָּה   חֲנֻכִּיָּה   נֵרוֹת

סֻכָּה   יְלָדִים   סֻכּוֹת   קִדוּשׁ   שַׁבָּת   חַלָּה

מַצּוֹת   פֶּסַח   הַגָּדָה   שָׁבוּעוֹת   חַג   תּוֹרָה

8 Now you know all the letters of the Alef-Bet.

In each group, in the words to the left of the line, circle the letter which appears on the right.

א   אַבָּא   אִמָּא   אָמֵן | ז   מְזוּזָה   מַזָּל   טוֹב

ב   בָּא   בָּאָה   בָּאִים | ח   חַלָּה   חַג   לֶחֶם

ג   הַגָּדָה   דָּג   חַג | ט   טוֹב   טוֹבָה   טַלִּית

ד   הַגָּדָה   קִדוּשׁ   יַלְדָּה | י   יַלְדָּה   אֲנִי   יוֹם

ה   הַמּוֹצִיא   חַלָּה   הַגָּדָה | כ   סֻכָּה   סֻכּוֹת   חֲנֻכָּה

ו   מִצְוָה   מִצְווֹת   מַצּוֹת | ל   חַלָּה   לֶחֶם   עֲלִיָּה

מ   מִי   שְׁמַע   מִצְוָה | צ   מַצָּה   מַצּוֹת   מִצְוָה

נ   נֵרוֹת   נֵר   חֲנֻכָּה | ק   קִדוּשׁ   מִקְדָּשׁ   הַשַּׁבָּת

ס   סִדוּר   סֻכָּה   סֻכּוֹת | ר   רֹאשׁ הַשָּׁנָה   פּוּרִים

ע   שָׁלוֹם עֲלֵיכֶם   עֲלִיָּה | שׁ   שָׁנָה   טוֹבָה   שַׁבָּת

פ   פֶּסַח   יוֹם כִּפּוּר | ת   תּוֹרָה   נֵרוֹת   סֻכּוֹת

9 You can do arithmetic with Hebrew letters.

100 = ק	40 = מ	7 = ז	1 = א
200 = ר	___ = נ	8 = ___	2 = ב
300 = שׁ	60 = ___	___ = ט	___ = ג
400 = ת	70 = ע	10 = י	4 = ד
	80 = פ	20 = כ	___ = ה
	___ = צ	___ = ל	6 = ו

$$\begin{array}{cccccc}
\textbf{נ} & \textbf{מ} & \textbf{ל} & \textbf{כ} & \textbf{ח} & \textbf{א} \\
-\,\textbf{מ} & -\,\textbf{י} & +\,\textbf{ו} & +\,\textbf{פ} & +\,\textbf{י} & +\,\textbf{ג} \\
\hline
\end{array}$$

10 Check the lines which are arranged in correct alphabetical order.

הַגָּדָה	דָּג	גָּדוֹל	בָּא	☐ אַבָּא
הַגָּדָה	גָּדוֹל	דָּג	אַבָּא	☐ בָּא
מִצְוָה	יַלְדָּה	לֶחֶם	טוֹבָה	☐ חַלָּה
מִצְוָה	לֶחֶם	יַלְדָּה	טוֹבָה	☐ חַלָּה

11 Look at the line of words below. After the first word, each word starts with the last letter of the word before it.

נֵרוֹת   תּוֹרָה   הַמּוֹצִיא   אֲנִי   יֶלֶד   דָּג   גָּדוֹל

Arrange the words on each line in the same way.

גָּדוֹל דָּג יֶלֶד	⟵	גָּדוֹל יֶלֶד דָּג

___	הַמּוֹצִיא		הַמּוֹצִיא חַלָּה אִמָּא
___	גָּדוֹל	___	גָּדוֹל חַג לֶחֶם
___	דָּג	___ מִי	יֶלֶד מִי גָּדוֹל דָּג

תּוֹרָה
Torah

The study of the Torah is an important part of the Jewish religion. When a child is born, the custom is to wish the newborn to grow up "to the study of תּוֹרָה, to marriage, and to good deeds."

In biblical times, on market days, the Torah was read aloud to the people. Even those who could not read were able to hear the reading of the תּוֹרָה.

Today, in the synagogue, we read the תּוֹרָה week by week. By the end of the year, the reading of the תּוֹרָה is completed.

On your בַּר מִצְוָה or בַּת מִצְוָה you are going to be honored with an Aliyah עֲלִיָה. You will join the reader of the תּוֹרָה at the pulpit. You may even read from the תּוֹרָה.

The custom is to chant a בְּרָכָה before the part of the תּוֹרָה is read and a second בְּרָכָה when the reading is finished.

Chanting adds feeling to the בְּרָכָה.

Here is the first בְּרָכָה said before the תּוֹרָה is read:

Blessed is	בָּרוּךְ אַתָּה
The Lord our God	אֲדֹנָי אֱלֹהֵינוּ
Ruler of the universe	מֶלֶךְ הָעוֹלָם
Who has chosen us	אֲשֶׁר בָּחַר בָּנוּ
From all people	מִכָּל הָעַמִּים
By giving us	וְנָתַן לָנוּ
His Torah	אֶת תּוֹרָתוֹ
Blessed is the Lord	בָּרוּךְ אַתָּה אֲדֹנָי
Giver of the Torah	נוֹתֵן הַתּוֹרָה

Letters Which Sound Alike

1 There are Hebrew letters which sound alike.

The letters ב and ו sound alike.

מַזָּל טוֹב   שָׁנָה טוֹבָה
מִצְוָה   אַבָּא וְאִמָּא   יֶלֶד וְיַלְדָּה

2 The letters שׂ and ס sound alike.

שְׁמַע יִשְׂרָאֵל   אֶרֶץ יִשְׂרָאֵל   חַג שָׂמֵחַ
סִדּוּר   חַג סֻכּוֹת   סֻכָּה   סֵפֶר תּוֹרָה

3 The letters ק and ___ sound alike.

חַג סֻכּוֹת   סֻכָּה   יוֹם כִּפּוּר   חֲנֻכָּה   חֲנֻכִּיָה
קָדוֹשׁ   מְקַדֵשׁ הַשַׁבָּת   אֲרוֹן הַקֹדֶשׁ   צַדִיקִים

4 The letters ת and ___ sound alike.

מַזָּל טוֹב   שָׁנָה טוֹבָה   טַלִית
תּוֹרָה   בַּת מִצְוָה   חַג הַסֻכּוֹת

5

Match the letters which sound alike.	Match the Final Letters.	Match the Sister Letters.
כּ ט	ם כ	כ ב
ת ק	ד מ	ב כּ
בּ ס	ץ נ	שׁ פּ
שׂ ו	ף פ	פ שׂ
		צ

אַ

father	אַבָּא בָּא	aba	אַבָּא
eats, m.	אַבָּא אוֹכֵל	ochel	אוֹכֵל
eat, pl.	הַיְלָדִים אוֹכְלִים	ochelim	אוֹכְלִים
eats, f.	הַיַלְדָה אוֹכֶלֶת	ochelet	אוֹכֶלֶת
mother	אִמָּא אוֹכֶלֶת	ima	אִמָּא
Amen	אָמֵן	Amen	אָמֵן
I	אֲנִי בָּא	ani	אֲנִי

בּ

comes, m.	אַבָּא בָּא	ba	בָּא
comes, f.	אִמָּא בָּאָה	ba'ah	בָּאָה
come, pl.	הַיְלָדִים בָּאִים	ba'im	בָּאִים
blessed	בָּרוּךְ אַתָּה אֲדֹנָי	baruch	בָּרוּךְ
blessing	בְּרָכָה	berachah	בְּרָכָה
blessings	בְּרָכוֹת	berachot	בְּרָכוֹת

גּ

big	יֶלֶד גָּדוֹל	gadol	גָּדוֹל

137

ד

| fish | דָּג גָּדוֹל | dag | דָּג |

ה

Havdalah	הַבְדָּלָה	Havdalah	הַבְדָּלָה
Haggadah	הַגָּדָה	Haggadah	הַגָּדָה
Hamotzi	הַמּוֹצִיא לֶחֶם	Hamotzi	הַמּוֹצִיא

ו

| and | וְ | ve | וְ |

ז

ח

holiday	חַג פּוּרִים	chag	חַג
room, school	חֶדֶר גָּדוֹל	cheder	חֶדֶר
chalah	חַלָּה יָפָה	chalah	חַלָּה
Chanukah	חַג חֲנֻכָּה	Chanukah	חֲנֻכָּה
Chanukiah or Chanukah menorah	חֲנֻכִּיָּה יָפָה	Chanukiah	חֲנֻכִּיָּה

138

Hebrew	Translit.	Example	English
טוֹב	tov	יֶלֶד טוֹב	good, m.
טוֹבָה	tovah	יַלְדָּה טוֹבָה	good, f.

י

Hebrew	Translit.	Example	English
יוֹם	yom	יוֹם כִּפּוּר	day
יוֹם כִּפּוּר	Yom Kippur	יוֹם כִּפּוּר	Yom Kippur
יֶלֶד	yeled	יֶלֶד גָּדוֹל	boy
יַלְדָּה	yaldah	יַלְדָּה בָּאָה	girl
יְלָדִים	yeladim	יְלָדִים בָּאִים	children, boys
יָפֶה	yafeh	חַג יָפֶה	nice, handsome, m.
יָפָה	yafah	יַלְדָּה יָפָה	nice, pretty, f.

כ

ל

Hebrew	Translit.	Example	English
לֹא	lo	לֹא גָּדוֹל	no, not
לֶחֶם	lechem	הַמּוֹצִיא לֶחֶם	bread

English	Example	Transliteration	Hebrew
			מ
who	מִי בַסֻּכָּה ?	mi	מִי
matzah	מַצָּה טוֹבָה	matzah	מַצָּה
good deed, mitzvah	מִצְוָה	mitzvah	מִצְוָה
mitzvot, good deeds	מִצְווֹת	mitzvot	מִצְווֹת
matzot	מַצּוֹת	matzot	מַצּוֹת
			נ
candle	נֵר וְחֲנֻכִּיָה	ner	נֵר
candles	נֵרוֹת וְחֲנֻכִּיָה	nerot	נֵרוֹת
			ס
prayer book	סִדּוּר יָפֶה	siddur	סִדּוּר
sukah	סֻכָּה יָפָה	sukah	סֻכָּה
Sukot	חַג הַסֻּכּוֹת	Sukot	סֻכּוֹת
			ע
Aliyah	עֲלִיָה	Aliyah	עֲלִיָה
			פ
Purim	חַג פוּרִים	Purim	פוּרִים
Passover	חַג הַפֶּסַח	Pesach	פֶּסַח

| pious man | צַדִיק גָדוֹל | tsadik | צַדִיק |
| pious men | צַדִיקִים | tsadikim | צַדִיקִים |

ק

| Kiddush | קִדוּש | Kiddush | קִדוּש |

ר

| Rosh Hashanah | רֹאשׁ הַשָׁנָה בָּא | Rosh Hashanah | רֹאשׁ הַשָׁנָה |

שׁ

Shabbat	שַׁבָּת שָׁלוֹם	Shabbat	שַׁבָּת
hello, goodbye, peace	שָׁלוֹם יְלָדִים	shalom	שָׁלוֹם
hear	שְׁמַע יִשְׂרָאֵל	Shema	שְׁמַע
year	שָׁנָה טוֹבָה	shanah	שָׁנָה

ת

| Torah | תּוֹרָה | Torah | תּוֹרָה |

The Creation of the Alef-Bet

When the world was about to be created, all the sounds and letters gathered around God in a huge circle. Each hoped that it would be chosen to be part of the Alef-Bet.

Some letters decorated themselves with beautiful crowns in order that God would notice their beauty.

Others stood humbly with their heads down, not daring to look up at the glory of God.

Some letters spoke proudly about their own importance and beauty. Others remained silent.

The שׁ spoke first:

> I should be first in the Alef-Bet. I have three beautiful crowns. I have the lovely sound Sh, Sh, the sound of a breeze blowing in the trees, the sound of running streams. I am the first letter in the word שָׁלוֹם. O God, You must create the world with שָׁלוֹם or it will be destroyed by wars.

God blessed the letter שׁ. He created peace with it—שָׁלוֹם. He created a day of rest and prayer with it—שַׁבָּת. But, most important, He created the word שְׁמַע to be used by His people whenever they wanted to pray to Him—שְׁמַע יִשְׂרָאֵל.

142

The letter ע spoke next and said:

Please choose me for your Alef-Bet. I will help You create Your עוֹלָם.

God liked the letter ע and picked it for the Alef-Bet.

Then came the letter מ who softly said:

There can be no world without מַיִם, no rain, no rivers, no seas. Without מַיִם for the land there will be no plants, no animals, no food for people.

And God liked the letter מ and put it in the middle of the Alef-Bet to be at the center of life.

He used the מ to separate the water from the land and give מַיִם to the earth.
He used the letter מ to create heaven שָׁמַיִם.
He also gave children the sound of מ so that they could call mother אִמָּא.

Then came another letter—slim, proud, and wearing a beautiful crown—the letter ז who said:

O God, make Your world a place for the brave. Make Your people strong and give them weapons with which to hunt.
Don't make Your world a place for the weak. Put me in the hands of those who will use me as a weapon and fight for You and Your תּוֹרָה.

God didn't like the words spoken by the letter ז. He didn't want his world to be a place of weapons and war. He was ready to let ז leave without joining the Alef-Bet. But then God asked Himself:

How will people be protected on earth? How will they fight wild animals without weapons? How will they hunt for food?

So God took the letter ז to be part of the Alef-Bet.

143

Next came the letter ט and spoke:

You must include me in the Alef-Bet for I am the first letter in all that is good טוֹב. Without טוֹב the world will be full of evil.

And God took the letter ט and put the word טוֹב in His creation. During the first six days of creating the world, He used טוֹב every day. The Bible says, in the story of the creation, that at the end of each day God looked around and said: "It is good כִּי טוֹב."

The letter ד was chosen because it stood for the word door דֶּלֶת. It told the people of the world: that God wanted those who had a lot to open their doors to those who did not have anything; that God wanted people to open their hearts to others; that God wanted men and women to open their ears to listen and their eyes to see—and understand.

The letter ל was chosen and made taller than all other letters to remind the people of Israel that learning לָמֵד should stand highest among the things they value.

Then God noticed that א and ב did not speak at all. "Why are you silent?" God asked. And א answered:

I am too low to deserve a special place. I am the first letter in the word אֲדָמָה earth. I am at the bottom of everybody's feet. I am the lowest of the low.

And God said: "Because you are humble, I'll make you the most important letter. You will be the first number אֶחָד. I will create the land אֲדָמָה with you and I'll put man אָדָם on it."

"And you, ב, the humblest of all letters, will be the first in my creation of the world בְּרֵאשִׁית בָּרָא."

144

There is none like our God
There is none like our Lord
There is none like our King
There is none like our Savior

אֵין כֵּאלֹהֵינוּ. אֵין כַּאדוֹנֵינוּ.
אֵין כְּמַלְכֵּנוּ. אֵין כְּמוֹשִׁיעֵנוּ.

Who is like our God?
Who is like our Lord?
Who is like our King?
Who is like our Savior?

מִי כֵאלֹהֵינוּ ? מִי כַאדוֹנֵינוּ ?
מִי כְמַלְכֵּנוּ ? מִי כְמוֹשִׁיעֵנוּ ?

We will give thanks to our God
We will give thanks to our Lord
We will give thanks to our King
We will give thanks to our Savior

נוֹדֶה לֵאלֹהֵינוּ. נוֹדֶה לַאדוֹנֵינוּ.
נוֹדֶה לְמַלְכֵּנוּ. נוֹדֶה לְמוֹשִׁיעֵנוּ.

Blessed is our God
Blessed is our Lord
Blessed is our King
Blessed is our Savior

בָּרוּךְ אֱלֹהֵינוּ. בָּרוּךְ אֲדוֹנֵינוּ.
בָּרוּךְ מַלְכֵּנוּ. בָּרוּךְ מוֹשִׁיעֵנוּ.

You are our God
You are our Lord
You are our King
You are our Savior

אַתָּה הוּא אֱלֹהֵינוּ. אַתָּה הוּא אֲדוֹנֵינוּ.
אַתָּה הוּא מַלְכֵּנוּ. אַתָּה הוּא מוֹשִׁיעֵנוּ.

תְּפִלָּה: אָבִינוּ מַלְכֵּנוּ

Our Father, our King

Be kind to us and answer when we call

Though we are lacking in good deeds

Help us with justice and charity

And save us

אָבִינוּ מַלְכֵּנוּ
חָנֵּנוּ וַעֲנֵנוּ
כִּי אֵין בָּנוּ מַעֲשִׂים
עֲשֵׂה עִמָּנוּ צְדָקָה וָחֶסֶד
וְהוֹשִׁיעֵנוּ

He is the eternal Lord who reigned before any being had yet been created

אֲדוֹן עוֹלָם אֲשֶׁר מָלַךְ
בְּטֶרֶם כָּל יְצִיר נִבְרָא

When all was done according to His will, already then His name was King

לְעֵת נַעֲשָׂה בְחֶפְצוֹ כֹּל
אֲזַי מֶלֶךְ שְׁמוֹ נִקְרָא

And after all has ceased to be, still will He reign in solitary majesty

וְאַחֲרֵי כִּכְלוֹת הַכֹּל
לְבַדּוֹ יִמְלוֹךְ נוֹרָא

He was, He is, and He will be in glory eternally

וְהוּא הָיָה וְהוּא הֹוֶה
וְהוּא יִהְיֶה בְּתִפְאָרָה

בִּרְכַּת הַמָּזוֹן

Here is part of בִּרְכַּת הַמָּזוֹן:

Blessed is the Lord our God

בָּרוּךְ אַתָּה אֲדֹנָי אֱלֹהֵינוּ

Ruler of the universe

מֶלֶךְ הָעוֹלָם

Your goodness supports the world

הַזָּן אֶת הָעוֹלָם כֻּלּוֹ בְּטוּבוֹ

With grace, with charity, with mercy

בְּחֵן בְּחֶסֶד וּבְרַחֲמִים

Blessed is the Lord

בָּרוּךְ אַתָּה אֲדֹנָי

Provider for all

הַזָּן אֶת הַכֹּל

146

| | מַה נִשְׁתַּנָּה |

| Why is this night different | מַה נִשְׁתַּנָּה הַלַּיְלָה הַזֶּה |
| From all other nights? | מִכָּל הַלֵּילוֹת ? |

On all other nights we may eat	שֶׁבְּכָל הַלֵּילוֹת אָנוּ אוֹכְלִין
Bread or matzah	חָמֵץ וּמַצָּה
But on this night only matzah	הַלַּיְלָה הַזֶּה כֻּלוֹ מַצָּה

On all other nights we may eat	שֶׁבְּכָל הַלֵּילוֹת אָנוּ אוֹכְלִין
Any kind of herbs	שְׁאָר יְרָקוֹת
But on this night only bitter herbs	הַלַּיְלָה הַזֶּה מָרוֹר

On all other nights we do not dip	שֶׁבְּכָל הַלֵּילוֹת אֵין אָנוּ מַטְבִּילִין
Even once	אֲפִילוּ פַּעַם אֶחָת
But on this night twice	הַלַּיְלָה הַזֶּה שְׁתֵּי פְעָמִים

On all other nights we may eat	שֶׁבְּכָל הַלֵּילוֹת אָנוּ אוֹכְלִין
Sitting up straight or leaning	בֵּין יוֹשְׁבִין וּבֵין מְסֻבִּין
This night we all lean	הַלַּיְלָה הַזֶּה כֻּלָנוּ מְסֻבִּין

| | הִנֵּה מַה טוֹב |

| It is good and pleasant | הִנֵּה מַה טוֹב וּמַה נָּעִים |
| For brothers to be together | שֶׁבֶת אַחִים גַּם יָחַד |

May He who has taught us the difference between the holy and the ordinary forgive us our sins

הַמַּבְדִּיל בֵּין קֹדֶשׁ לְחוֹל
חַטֹּאתֵינוּ הוּא יִמְחוֹל

May He increase our people and our welfare like the sand and like the stars at night

זַרְעֵנוּ וְכַסְפֵּנוּ יַרְבֶּה כַּחוֹל
וְכַכּוֹכָבִים בַּלַּיְלָה

May it be a good week

שָׁבוּעַ טוֹב, שָׁבוּעַ טוֹב

May it be a good week

שָׁבוּעַ טוֹב, שָׁבוּעַ טוֹב

דָּוִד מֶלֶךְ יִשְׂרָאֵל

David, king of Israel
Lives on forever

דָּוִד מֶלֶךְ יִשְׂרָאֵל
חַי חַי וְקַיָּם

שֶׁהֶחֱיָנוּ

We give thanks to You
O Lord our God
Ruler of the universe
For giving us life
For sustaining us
And for enabling us to reach this day of joy
Amen

בָּרוּךְ אַתָּה
אֲדֹנָי אֱלֹהֵינוּ
מֶלֶךְ הָעוֹלָם
שֶׁהֶחֱיָנוּ
וְקִיְּמָנוּ
וְהִגִּיעָנוּ לַזְּמַן הַזֶּה
אָמֵן

Sample Bingo Card

הָ	דָ	גִ	פְ	אָ
פֵ	אֵ	חָ	וָ	וָ
יֵ	הֵ	░░░	דֵ	גֵ
גֵ	פֵ	אָ	חֵ	וֵ
חֵ	וֵ	וֵ	הֵ	דֵ

On page 151, you will find the squares containing Hebrew sounds which you are to cut out to make your own Bingo card. On page 153, you will find the squares containing Hebrew words to make another Bingo card.

Cut out the sounds arranged in the squares below. Mix the squares well, choose any 24 and glue them on a large piece of paper to make your own Bingo card.

הָ	דָ	גָ	בָּ	אָ
בֶּ	אֶ	חָ	זָ	וָ
זֶ	וֶ	הֶ	דֶ	גֶ
דְ	גְ	בְּ	אְ	חֶ
אוֹ	חְ	זְ	וְ	הְ
זוֹ	הוֹ	דוֹ	גוֹ	בּוֹ

151

Cut out the words arranged in the squares below. Mix the words very well and choose 24. You will then have a Bingo card.

יְלָדִים	יַלְדָּה	יֶלֶד	אִמָּא	אַבָּא
נֵרוֹת	נֵר	בָּאִים	בָּאָה	בָּא
אוֹכְלִים	אוֹכֶלֶת	אוֹכֵל	לֶחֶם	חַלָּה
בְּרָכוֹת	בְּרָכָה	אֲנִי	חֲנֻכִּיָּה	חֲנֻכָּה
מִי	חַג	עֲלִיָּה	סִדּוּר	אָמֵן
סֻכּוֹת	סֻכָּה	עוֹלָם	הַבְדָּלָה	הַגָּדָה
מְזוּזָה	יוֹם טוֹב	יוֹם	גָּדוֹל	פֶּסַח
בָּרוּךְ	טוֹבָה	טוֹב	מַזָּל טוֹב	דָּג

153